Karma is Negotiable

Karma is Negotiable
Destiny and the Divine Power of Love

by Nikias Annas

GLORIAN

Karma is Negotiable
A Glorian Book / 2011
First Edition

© 2011 Glorian Publishing

ISBN 978-1-934206-52-2

Glorian Publishing is a non-profit organization dedicated
to aiding humanity to overcome suffering through the
application of Gnosis: conscious, experiential knowledge.
All proceeds go to further the distribution of these books.
For more information, visit:

gnosticteachings.org

Contents

Illustrations

Introduction

Everyone experiences suffering. Obviously, death and physical pain are forms of suffering. Yet, we also suffer from an incredible variety of emotional, mental, and spiritual afflictions. We suffer when we do not have what we want, and we suffer once we have what we want, because we are afraid of losing it. We suffer from change, both from the changes we do not want, which occur anyway, and the changes we do want, that do not occur. For us, life is a constant fluctuation of uncertainty, and suffering is a common companion.

Much of what we human beings pursue in life is but an attempt to avoid or lessen our suffering. Ultimately, however, unless we deal directly with the very causes of suffering, it will never be overcome. This is because of a simple law of nature: cause and effect. Suffering occurs because of causes—that is, specific actions that create specific results.

The fact is that suffering can be overcome, but not through materialism. No matter how wealthy or famous a person may become, they still suffer, often suffering more than those with "less."

To change the phenomena of suffering, one must work with very fundamental forces of nature. These forces are not influenced at all by our beliefs, intentions, or hopes. They are forces in nature, and thus to work with them, one must act.

This book is about action, not theory or belief. To understand this book, you must put it into action in your daily life, living and working with the principles it presents, in order to verify through your own experience the knowledge that is being communicated. Without a continual effort to experience these teachings in one's own life, this knowledge will remain as nothing more than ephemeral phantoms in the intellect, which can render no service for the betterment of your soul. Yet, for those who make moment to moment effort to consciously transform their experience of life, many new doors will open to them. They learn from experience that suffering can be exchanged for happiness and genuine contentment.

"A wise person is one who, having accurately analyzed all actions of body, speech, and mind, always acts for the benefit of self and others."

- Nagarjuna, Precious Garland

Cause and Effect

The modern way of thinking assumes that everything that exists has a cause. This is the basic idea behind science: causality, or the relationship between cause and effect.

Cause and effect is not a theory or a belief, it is a law. As a law, it does not matter if you have heard of it, believe in it, or ignore it. Everything about you is subject to the law of cause and effect.

Laws manage everything that exists, and there is no more fundamental law than cause and effect.

Even gravity is a minor law in comparison with cause and effect. A few miles above the surface of the Earth, the power of gravity begins to fade. Yet cause and effect has no such boundary. It manages every existing thing, on every level, from the subatomic to universes.

Everything that exists depends upon cause and effect. There are no exceptions to cause and effect, though there are many cases where we lack the ability to perceive particular causes. Nonetheless, the law of cause and effect is universal.

According to all of our most ancient traditions, the universe arises and falls in cycles of birth and death. Just as we have days and nights, and seasons, all existing objects pass through cycles. On the scale of the universe, there are cosmic days and nights, great periods of birth, existence, death, and repose. Throughout the birth and death of worlds, suns, and cosmic systems, cause and effect is the law that balances everything. In other words, existence happens because of cause and effect. Without this law of cause and effect, existence would not be possible.

Yet, the law of cause and effect is not fixed or rigid like some kind of predetermined story, "fate," or "destiny," because such a law can only be set in motion when the conditions allow. A simple example is in the striking of a match to create a flame; without conducive conditions, the match will not light, such as underwater or if there is no oxygen. Likewise, on every level of existence, the conditions must be right for this law to be rendered active.

In traditions like Buddhism and Hinduism, which have studied this subject in great depth, the law of cause and effect is known as "karma." The actual meaning of karma is poorly understood in the West, where people commonly associated it with some kind of debt to the universe or God. The real meaning of the Sanskrit term karma is "cause and effect," or "action and consequence." Karma is derived from the root word karman, which means "an act." Every act is a cause for specific results. Thus, karma is just this: action and its consequences. Understanding this, we can naturally see that actions that produce beneficial consequences are just as "karmic" as actions that produce harm.

Nowadays, many people respond to this topic by leaping to its implications for the creation of the universe, or how it applies to natural catastrophes and other unique but interesting situations. While such subjects may be very compelling for debate or discussion, as they are currently beyond our ability to truly confirm or disprove, they are merely theoretical, and a merely theoretical or scholarly point of view is not very useful in daily life. Having an opinion or theory about the origin of mankind or the beginning of existence does not do much at all to help us with the problems that are afflicting us right now. Therefore, let us first understand karma personally, in our own life, as this kind of knowledge can render great changes that we can experience for ourselves.

Through action, we create results. Everything that we are now is a result of actions already taken. To be that which we aspire to be, we have to know what actions we need to take in order to produce the results we want. Moreover, we need to establish the conditions within which those actions, those causes, can bear fruit.

The human being has an infinite potential, yet to develop it one must know how. Nothing in the universe arises by chance or by a predetermined fate. Everything arises due to causes and conditions. To become a fully developed human being, we must perform the actions that engender such results. To do that, we have to understand exactly how karma works, and how to master it.

The first step then, is to reflect on our own experience with the four fundamentals of cause and effect.

1. The Certainty of Cause and Effect

Much—if not all—suffering occurs because of ignorance about cause and effect. By ignorance we do not mean a lack of book study or intellectual understanding, but to a lack of real knowledge. Real knowledge is cognizant knowledge. One only has to be burned one time to acquire genuine knowledge of the power of fire or heat. From then on, that knowledge cannot be ignored. Even if one has a strong desire whose fulfillment requires being burned (such as retrieving a cherished object from a raging fire), it is unlikely that one will be willing to be burned. And certainly, one would not take such pain for something unimportant.

Unfortunately, we lack this kind of knowledge regarding almost everything in life. We may believe it is wrong to lie, and though we have experienced the pain of being lied to, we continue to lie to others and to ourselves, because of ignorance: a lack of real knowledge—cognizant knowledge—of the consequences of lying.

A drunkard knows that alcohol is bad for him, but he continues to drink because he lacks cognizance—real knowledge— of the consequences of his drinking. Even having lost everything important to him in life—his family, career, social standing—he will continue to drink, because his desire is greater than his knowledge. In other words, he has not yet realized the inevitable relationship between action and consequence. He has no cognizance of karma.

For every action, there is a result. No matter how small or insignificant an action may seem, it will have consequences, even if we are unaware of them.

By actions, we mean not only what we say or do with our bodies, but also what we think and feel. Our internal actions can impact our external environment. The way we think and feel can be sensed by others, and can change their attitude towards us.

How many people have not been hired for a job, because the employer could sense the negative thoughts or feelings of the applicant? Even a well-qualified person will be rejected if they give off a bad atmosphere. An astute employer can sense a thief, a liar, or a person who cannot be trusted. There is no physical evidence for these impressions, but they are perceptible, because of our psychological environment. The state of our psychology can be sensed by others, thus what we think and feel has consequences.

How many good women have sensed the terrible, secret lust of an otherwise decent man, thus he remains alone? He may never show his lust externally, and only indulge in it in his mind, yet others can sense it.

What we think and feel, though it is "inside of us," has an external impact that we generally ignore. Thus, our actions, whether internal or external, have effects.

Reflect on your own actions every day. Reflect on any action you intend to pursue. Be sure you have weighed the impact of every act, for once performed, it cannot be erased.

In every area of life, it is essential to recognize the certainty of cause and effect. Even if we do not immediately see

the consequences of an action, the consequences will inevitably arrive as soon
as the conditions are conducive—unless
a more powerful action overpowers their
emergence. We will talk more about this
later.

Additionally, though we are not
always able to perceive the relationship
between cause and effect, it does not
mean the relationship does not exist.
However, it often happens that we do
have the ability to see it, but we do not
want to; much of the time, we are unwilling to see the truth. We prefer to maintain
our illusions.

2. Effects Are Greater Than the Cause

Although most people think that an
action produces an equal consequence,
that is not true. A tiny seed grows into a
plant many times larger, which produces
more seeds and more plants. Thus, the
original action—the seed—produces truly
awesome results. Likewise, our actions
develop consequences that are greater
than the action.

A very simple example is to imagine throwing a stone into a pond. Most people think of cause and effect as merely being the relationship between the throw and the splash of water. Yet, when analyzed, there is much more occurring. The energy required to throw a stone is rather small, yet the impact of the stone results in a distribution of energy that is far, far greater than the original expenditure of energy. The splash is but the result of the initial impact of the stone on the water. But what about the waves created by the impact? On a still pond, the waves can extend for a very long distance, disturbing the entire pond; not just on the surface, but also towards the bottom, as well as any fish, plants, or other organisms, who might be terrified or disturbed. Moreover, such an action is not limited to just the material consequences; the sound also travels a long distance and creates an impact in a wide area.

Correspondingly, every action we perform has waves of impact that flow both outward and inward. Every action we perform also affects us inside, psychologically.

Numerous psychological problems (inside of us) are caused by the cumulative results of negative actions we performed externally. Yet, because we have never learned to pay attention to our actions and their effects, we are deeply ignorant of the full power of our actions.

The consequences are always greater than the action. This is true for negative actions and positive ones. If we plant the seeds of nourishing fruit, we can feed many people, for generations. Yet if we plant the seeds of selfishness, anger, or lust, we can originate harm on a scale that we can scarcely imagine.

How much greater the effects are than the originating action depends upon the conditions surrounding the action. A word spoken in solitude does not have much effect. But the same word spoken at just the right moment, in the right place, can change the world. In every case, the power of an action is determined by the conditions that surround it. Thus, it is necessary to not only contemplate well the type of action we want to perform, but the precise conditions needed to facilitate it. For instance, many people attempt to educate their children by relentlessly stating the same instructions over and over, yet the child continues to ignore the advice. To truly influence a child in the right way, those words could be spoken one time, if one knows the precise moment to do so.

3. You cannot receive the consequence without committing its corresponding action.

Actions produce corresponding consequences.

It is obvious that on the physical level in order to be nourished, you must eat. To live, you must breathe. To be clean, you must bathe. Similarly, to have spiritual insight, you must see for yourself; no one can do it for you.

Everything in nature works according to laws. Our spiritual development is subject to laws also.

Many people are deeply hypnotized by the desire to get something for nothing. Everyone wants to win the lottery or "strike it rich" without having to work for wealth. This is a foolish fantasy that originates enormous suffering. The fact is that nothing is free, and everyone receives exactly what they deserve, according to the causes they originated in the past.

> "Be not deceived; God is not mocked: for whatsoever a man soweth, that shall he also reap." - Galatians 6:7

In other words, whatever we have in life, we earned. Whatever we do not have, we have not earned.

If we want happiness, we have to produce the causes for happiness. If we want freedom, we have to produce the causes for freedom. That is, we originate our own future through our present actions.

Thus, it is wise to consider the consequences of each action we perform. What will be created by our anger? Certainly, anger cannot create peace, understanding, or contentment. Anger can only create anger, pain, and resentment. Angry people spread their anger to everyone else in their environment, and receive much more anger in return. Imagine an angry bus driver. The angry bus driver treats all the passengers poorly, thus everyone responds to the driver with irritation, anger, sarcasm, all of which naturally makes the bus driver more angry. A cycle is put in motion, and it feeds itself daily, getting stronger. A person who lives like this has a life filled with bitterness and complaints, always directed at others, blaming "the system" or "management"—but it all originated from themselves. Many people live their entire lives this way, whether with perpetuated anger, envy, lust, or other harmful qualities. Thus, such a person can never have what they want—respect, peace, contentment—because they had never acted in a way that resulted in those consequences.

You know it is true: if you smile at others, they smile back. This is karma in motion. Yet, mere "knowing it is true" is not the same as living it. We "know" many truths, but do not have cognizance of them. Cognizance is proven by our actions. If you want certain conditions in your life, you have to perform the actions that will create them. Suffering cannot be overcome through creating more suffering, yet that is what we attempt. Suffering can only be overcome by stopping the actions that create it.

4. Once an action is performed, the consequence cannot be erased.

Many people like to believe that they can "take back" mistaken acts, or have them "forgiven," but it is an undeniable law that whatever is done is done, and cannot be painted over.

A hurtful word will change a relationship forever. Similarly, a moment of sincere generosity can change a life forever.

A child who encounters pornography will be forever changed. The images of lust will change the psychology of that child.

A child who experiences violence will never be the same. No matter how peaceful and fruitful the rest of that child's life, the experience of violence can never be erased from the psyche.

Similarly, everything we do is permanent. The depth and influence of every action depends on many factors, but no action can ever be erased.

Nature has a type of memory that is eternal. So do we, but we ignore it.

Fortunately, any harmful action and its consequences can be overpowered. As grave as our suffering and problems may be, karma is also the power that can transform them into happiness.

A superior law always overcomes an inferior one.

A stronger action overcomes a weaker one. This is the key to genuine happiness.

Through understanding how to utilize karma (action and consequence), all suffering can be overcome. Yes—all suffering.

Every enlightened being—no matter what name we use for them—reached that state by means of this fact: any circumstance (which is a result of previous actions) can be changed by performing superior actions. This is how we can understand the forbearance and incredible strength of all of our greatest spiritual examples: Jesus, Buddha, Krishna, Milarepa, Moses, Joan of Arc, and others. Their power to overcome adversity and suffering was rooted in a profound understanding of cause and effect: knowing how to perform the right action at the right moment in the right circumstances.

This kind of accurate knowledge and its results are accessible to an awakened consciousness. By learning how to use our consciousness, we learn how to direct energy towards the circumstances we need. By discarding harmful actions and adopting beneficial ones, we can transform life.

The Origin Affects the Outcome

Some traditions understand that the physical world is side-by-side with many other dimensions or levels of reality. Even modern science realizes the certainty of levels of existence that we cannot perceive directly, thus to see some of them we need special tools, like microscopes, telescopes, x-ray devices, and many other extensions of our physical senses.

Even merely at the physical level, light has many degrees of vibration. With our physical senses we only perceive an extremely narrow band of that vibration, and cannot directly perceive the vast majority of the light that is radiating around us right now. To some degree, we can perceive the results of action in the narrow band of physical action. However, we do not perceive the results of action in the expanse of the ultraviolet and infrared regions. All the vibrations of light inter-penetrate without confusion.

At this moment, you are surrounded by light corresponding to every range of vibration. When you move your hand, you see the physical action and its results. But you do not see your hand moving in the ultraviolet, and you do not see your hand moving in the infrared. Yet beyond the physical level of matter and energy, there are huge expanses of reality that we cannot perceive with physical tools. To see them we need special tools. Here we do not refer to physical technologies, which are merely an extension of the physical senses: we refer to psychological technologies, which traditionally are called meditation, clairvoyance, and dream yoga or astral projection. Few are they that learn the proper use of these techniques, and indeed you know you have been properly trained when you have the ability to retrieve information from non-physical levels of life.

This is important, because our actions have results throughout the range of worlds. The movement of your hand produces results that you cannot perceive with the physical senses. Your words and thoughts produce movements of energy that are not physical. There are other—much greater—consequences that are unseen by our physical senses.

Cause and effect is at work in the physical world according to the laws of physical matter. It is different in the internal worlds. What happens internally—psychologically, spiritually—is more powerful.

The internal worlds are those aspects of nature that we cannot perceive with our physical senses. In other words, we are multidimensional, not just physical.

The Tibetan Buddhist master Tsong Khapa wrote,

> "An effect of immense happiness may arise from even a small virtuous karma [act]. An effect of immense suffering may arise from even a tiny nonvirtuous karma [act]. Hence, internal causation seems to involve a magnification that is not found in external causation." - Tsong Khapa, Lamrim Chenmo

In other words, a deed may be small, but its effects can be great, and this is especially true of those actions produced internally—that is, psychologically and consciously.

In modern physics, it is now known that two objects at remote physical distance from one another can have a pro-

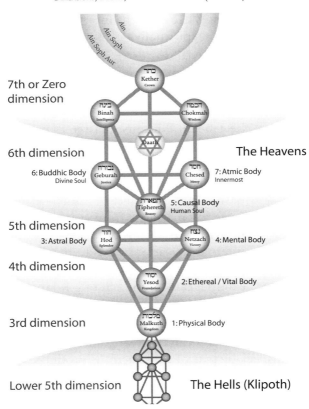

DIMENSIONS, BODIES, AND THE TREE OF LIFE (KABBALAH)

Ain
Ain Soph
Ain Soph Aur

7th or Zero dimension

כתר
Kether
Crown

בינה
Binah
Intelligence

חכמה
Chokmah
Wisdom

Daath

6th dimension

The Heavens

6: Buddhic Body
Divine Soul

גבורה
Geburah
Justice

חסד
Chesed
Mercy

7: Atmic Body
Innermost

תפארת
Tiphereth
Beauty

5: Causal Body
Human Soul

5th dimension

3: Astral Body

הוד
Hod
Splendor

נצח
Netzach
Victory

4: Mental Body

4th dimension

יסוד
Yesod
Foundation

2: Ethereal / Vital Body

3rd dimension

מלכות
Malkuth
Kingdom

1: Physical Body

Lower 5th dimension

The Hells (Klipoth)

found and intimate energetic interaction. This is due to multidimensionality. Of course, spiritual and mystical traditions have always known this, even though the majority of humanity ignores it.

We are not merely physical; we are multidimensional.

Our physical body corresponds to the third dimension, and this includes everything we can perceive with the senses of our physical body. Yet, our physical body can only exist and perceive because of the energy that empowers it. That energy belongs to the fourth dimension. Some people can sense this energy, but not with physical senses. Some people call this energy chi or prana. It is vital energy, the basis of physical life.

Further, our body is animated by more than mere vital energy: we have psychic, mental, and emotional energy, which are related to the fifth dimension. This is what we commonly experience as the world of dreams. While we can sense our thoughts and feelings from the physical world, they actually exist in another level of nature.

All of that experience—physical, vital, emotional, mental—is made possible because of our consciousness, soul, and spirit, which vibrate in the sixth dimension.

All of these levels emerge from and return to the seventh or zero dimension, what Buddhist call Emptiness, and Kabbalists call Ain ("nothingness").

In simple terms, even though we are here physically (third dimension), we experience the effects of having vital energy (fourth dimension). Our physical senses may not be able to "see" it, but when our vital energy is low we feel tired or depleted. We also experience the effects of psychic energy, our thoughts and feelings (fifth dimension). Though we cannot physically "see" these thoughts and feelings, we can perceive them, just not with our physical senses.

In every moment, we are utilizing all of these forms of energy, and all of them are producing consequences.

Right now, your actions are creating multidimensional effects. But, you cannot see them because your consciousness is asleep. If you awaken your consciousness, then you can see other dimensions.

As Tsong Khapa pointed out, actions produced psychologically (internally) have much greater effects than those produced physically (externally). This is partly because the physical realm is quite low on the scale of matter and energy. Moving up the scale, actions have greater consequences, because they "trickle down" to the lower levels.

For example, if we "mouth" a word, simulating the saying of the word but without actually speaking it; this will have only a negligible effect. Yet if we say it, pronouncing the word aloud, this means we used vital energy to propel the body and the breath. The result then is that the word makes a sound, and the effect is thereby greater. But if we say the word with emotion, and direct it by thought, and especially direct it by conscious will, the effect of that word can be devastating or life-changing. The higher the type of energy invested, the greater the effect. When we say something that we really mean, it is because all of these energies are empowering that word. That is why such words are so powerful. The same is true of all forms of action. The more we mean it, the more powerful the action becomes.

Additionally, as we have stated, each action creates an effect that is greater than the original action. Even though Newton explained that cause and effect are equal ("For every action there is an equal and opposite reaction"), this only applies to isolated systems in the third dimension (physical matter and energy). The reality is that nothing is merely physical. Modern physics has already realized this, but most people have not.

Every physical action has ripple effects, not only physically, but in other dimensions. Thus, the results are far greater than the action.

Dimensions are not somewhere else, far away from us; the other dimensions are right here, right now. Although we possess senses that can perceive those dimensions, in us, those senses are atrophied. That is, we are asleep. We need to awaken. When we awaken, we can experience those dimensions as easily as we experience the physical one. Through such experience, we can directly observe for ourselves that a thought has a powerful ripple effect that flows into other dimensions or levels of energy and matter.

Thoughts are not isolated in our brains. Thoughts are a form of matter and energy that are not physical. Very sensitive people (and children and animals) can perceive the thoughts of others.

Most people can "sense" when someone is looking at them, even without physical clues. Have you felt the gaze of someone fall upon you, and you "instinctively" turned to see who is looking at you? In that moment, you sensed something by means of non-physical energy. You sensed the other persons attention, which is not physical.

Similarly, we can sense how others feel. A person may be smiling, but we can sense their anger or sadness. This is derived from non-physical energies and non-physical senses. In spite of this, we foolishly believe that no one else can sense what we are feeling or thinking. How naive!

Recognizing this, it is imperative that we realize something: what we think and feel have effects that extend far beyond the thought or feeling. What we **will** has far-reaching consequences. Everything inside of us produces consequences, both internally and externally.

This is why the Buddhist scripture *The Dhammapada* begins with:

> "The mind creates our life. As we think, so do we become."

Our life is but the result of the energy that has moved through our psyche. Thus, if what we want is a better life, we have to develop the capacity to change how we manage our energy. To do that, we need to become aware of ourselves here and now. The key to conquering suffering and establishing happiness is in this: being conscious of what we do both physically and internally, from moment to moment. Through conscious (superior) actions, we overcome unconscious (inferior) actions and their consequences.

Everything is Karmic

Karma, cause and effect, is universal and all-penetrating. Like contemplating infinity, the true meaning of the law of karma is elusive to the mind. The true activity of this law, the reality of this law, is something that our tiny mind cannot comprehend; yet, even though the mind cannot comprehend this, our consciousness can understand it, intuitively.

The law of karma is real; it is the very fabric of the entire existence around you and within you. You yourself are a result of karma, and everything you think, feel, and do creates a result, which, as we know, is the very definition of karma.

You may think you can understand this. You may think, "Yes, I understand that karma is the law of cause and effect and that if I do something bad then something bad will happen to me." Yes, that is true. If you hurt someone, then you will hurt. It is the function of the law to balance all action. The law of karma is the law of the scale. This law is present in everything; for everything we do there is a reaction, a response. Indeed, perhaps some of us DO get this, and we try to behave well, but the true depth of this law, the profound reach of this law, is something that none of us truly understand, because if we did, we would not live the way we do.

How different would our lives be if we really understood that everything we think creates karma? Every single thought that enters into our mind, that processes in our mind has a profound effect... So do our feelings, intentions, fantasies, as well as our physical actions. If we truly understood that our thoughts and feelings affect others and ourselves—usually with harm—we would make the sincere effort to instead generate beneficial thoughts and feelings.

Each and every thought we have engenders a consequence. Our thinking is creating something. Our out-of-control mind, that runs and thinks and considers and imagines without control and without awareness is generating a constant stream of energy that will inevitably have some effect. Moreover, according to the laws of nature, that effect will be greater than the cause.

Our every use of energy, on every level of our psyche, has an effect much greater than the action that produced it. However, at the moment, we do not see the effect. We are in a state of ignorance. That is, we are asleep.

> "Awake thou that sleepest, and arise from the [spiritually] dead, and Christ shall give thee light [in your consciousness]." - Ephesians 5:14

How We Know
Karma is Real

If we only think of karma as a theory, this type of teaching can never benefit us. If we only think of karma on a cosmic scale (such as debating the creation of worlds, or worrying over the role of God, etc), then we will waste a lot of time on questions that are beyond our ability to answer with certainty. Remember, we need cognizant knowledge, not theories. Without real experience of how karma works and the subsequent wisdom that emerges from that knowledge, our life will continue as it has: marching with uncertainty and anxiety towards death.

It is easy to experience the reality of karma. You can test it every day. All you have to do is pay attention to the effects of your actions.

If we do something to benefit someone else, we also benefit. For example, in the short term, we benefit from the emotions we feel, from the gratitude or reward we receive from others. In the long term, we may gain more. Yet, if we do something harmful, we are also harmed; in the short term, by regret, anxiety, the fear of retribution or punishment, etc. In the long term, we may receive more negative consequences.

Thus, through the analysis of what both we are doing, and the results of those actions, we begin to realize how karma works. This requires sincere self-analysis, from moment to moment, and from day to day. To succeed in this analysis, it is necessary that we are truly objective in our observations; that is, impartial. We have to see the facts, and stop justifying the actions of ourselves or others.

Going deeper, by analyzing our current situation, we can determine the previous actions that created it. Success in this effort requires special skills that we will discuss later.

Begin by observing yourself constantly. From moment to moment, be aware of the thoughts, feelings, and impulses that emerge within you. This is not easy to do, nor to sustain, because our consciousness is weak and untrained. Yet, by learning how to energize the consciousness (through special teachings hidden in every religion, and taught publicly by teachers like Samael Aun Weor) and direct it from moment to moment, we can start to consciously experience the deep relationship between our inner state and the external events around us.

Success in gathering conscious self-knowledge depends upon three irreplaceable factors:

1. Accurate training in the technique and supporting tools
2. The willpower to put it into activity from moment to moment
3. The patience to overcome obstacles and see results

We define training as being accurate when the student is capable of acquiring information through their own, personal implementation of that training. If the student is not acquiring information, then either they have not been trained well, they are not bothering to make the effort, or there is a karmic debt that is preventing the student from succeeding.

Some traditions call this technique self-observation and self-remembering. Others call it watchfulness, mindfulness, or awareness. Quite simply, it is to be here and now, observant of oneself. This is a state of consciousness marked by simple presence, aware, bright and clear, perceptive, receptive, and insightful. It is not a state of daydreaming, fantasizing, remembering, avoiding, desiring, craving, or ignoring.

By application of conscious attention, we can start to see how what we experience is related to what we have done. When we become deeply aware of how painful anger is, we will not want to be angry anymore. Indeed, we will seek a different way to deal with our frustrations. Similarly, each phenomena in our inner and outer life can reveal a way out of the cage we have built around ourselves, but to see the way out, we have to learn to look. We have to be willing to see the truth.

Our Present Reality

It takes a lot of willpower to develop the activity of our consciousness, because our consciousness is asleep. It may feel exhausting to bring the consciousness to present awareness and to direct it: to consciously observe. In the beginning, this requires a very rigorous, strong, tiring effort. If your spirituality is flaccid, weak, ephemeral—you just sort of float along through life—then you are working in the wrong way. Real spiritual development does not occur by just being on autopilot. All the myths that describe this path emphasize the unbelievable heroic efforts that the heroes have to make in order to save the maiden, to dominate the monster or dragon—real spirituality requires incredible sacrifice, work, and is dangerous. Those are not just pretty fairy tales; they reflect a living, vibrating truth: our consciousness is asleep and in danger, and to awaken it requires every ounce of strength we have.

For that effort we need an enormous amount of energy. That is why all genuine religions have harnessed the power of the sexual energy to fuel spiritual awakening. Beginners in every religion were required to conserve their sexual energy, so that energy could be converted into spiritual power.

Awakening does not come through concepts in the intellect, or beliefs in the heart, or repeated actions in the body. Awakening comes through energizing and activating the consciousness.

Liberation from suffering does not come through intentions, the way we dress, the way we talk or the books we read. Liberation comes as a result of—right now—paying attention, being awake and aware of the consciousness itself, and freeing ourselves from the causes of suffering. Those who awaken the consciousness without freeing themselves from pride, anger, lust, envy, gluttony and all those selfish desires become terrible sources of suffering for themselves and others.

In order to empower the consciousness, it is necessary to save our energy and to give it to the consciousness; then, we must learn to direct it towards the goal of liberation from the causes of suffering.

As Buddha Shakyamuni explained in the Four Noble Truths, suffering is caused by desire. Thus, we learn to pay attention to desire in all its forms, to learn how it functions, and to see the results of its activity.

Our consciousness in its original, natural state, is free, happy, wise, and capable of seeing the Divine. Yet, over the centuries, we have trapped that consciousness in pride, lust, envy, fear, greed, laziness, etc., thus our consciousness is modified by those qualities. We can no longer see the Divine. That is why we have so many theories and beliefs. We no longer have conscious knowledge of the Divine. To restore the natural state of the consciousness, we have to remove the obscurations. We cannot remove them if we cannot see them.

It is one thing to pay attention to what is going on outside of us, and this is good; we have to pay attention to our environment. Yet it is another thing to pay attention to what is happening in the intellect. This is also important—to watch our thoughts. It is something else to consciously watch our feelings, our emotions. And it is something else again to observe the sensations and impulses of the body and how we react to them. Observing all of these elements is fundamental to the process of developing conscious self-observation. But really, to awaken consciousness and reach freedom from suffering, we need to be aware of the consciousness itself—how we perceive. How—not just the fact of perception, but how we are perceiving. This is a supercritical action for us to observe, because every action of body, speech, and mind requires consciousness.

Then, once we learn to be aware of the activity of consciousness, we have to also see: is our consciousness modified by desires, or is it free, unrestricted? Most of the time we have no idea what the motivations for our actions are, because we are not paying attention. We are usually so overwhelmed with the surging chaos of thoughts, worries, concerns, fears, and desires that we have no self-cognizance in the midst of it. We are like a log tossed on a stormy sea. That stormy sea is our mind, and we are tossed about by all the surging wills in our minds. Inside, we are experiencing a surging, psychological chaos. Even when it subsides, we remain in psychological darkness, without any real sense of why we are alive.

To just go along with the circumstances of life, to just be tossed around by the competing desires within us, is to allow oneself to go down the drain, because really, everything on this planet— all of the energy, all of the forces—are going down the drain. It is not hard to see it. Unfortunately, we do not want to see it; we prefer to avoid seeing the truth of what is happening in the world.

If you want to be free from suffering and develop your fullest capacities, you cannot just sit back and relax, and tell yourself that you are "spiritual" or "okay," and let the current of life take you. If you want to do that, it is your choice, but are you sure of where the current of life is going? When you consider the basic aspects of karma which we have spoken about and apply them to the world as a whole, you can see that all of the actions of humanity have set in motion a huge storm of energy, driven by anger, greed, lust, jealousy, fear, gluttony, and more, whose results will be an unimaginable deepening of the suffering we are already enduring. It would be wise to learn how to escape this situation, and to help others do the same.

To incarnate wisdom, to become truly wise, we have to change, and change does not come by sitting back. Change comes through work, and not merely a little bit of effort, not just a few minutes a day, but a continual effort. Think about this example: you are shipwrecked, holding on to your log — that log is your life, your circumstances in life, that which keeps you afloat, your family, job, and situation. All of us, at any instant, right now, could lose everything, because nothing in this world is stable. At any instant, everything we have could be taken away. If you do not believe me, ask somebody in the any of the countries that has recently experienced a disaster or war. They will tell you that suddenly, from one moment to the next, everything you have relied upon is gone. None of us have any assurance that what we have now will be here tomorrow. Thus, we need to be serious about developing something we can rely upon. That will not be outside of us, but inside of us.

We are on the little raft of our life, and the current is taking us; how are we going to swim out of the whirlpool that is sucking the world into chaos? With all of that energy that is pulling all of us, how will you get out of it? Are you truly going to sit on your log and read a book and expect that you will avoid pain and suffering? Do you sincerely expect that a religious belief will free you from suffering? Have you not seen all the believers who suffer as much as non-believers? Do you know anyone who has been saved from suffering by a theory?

Only action can save us from destruction. To escape the destructive current of life, you have to swim with all of your might, with every ounce of energy that you have. You have to fight the current of life. That current is outside of you, and it is inside of you. The way to fight the current is to analyze yourself, and change. It sounds desperate, because it is. Our situation truly is desperate.

Some say that we must rely on God or the Divine to help us. While there is truth in this statement, it is equally true that unless we do our part, there is nothing the Divine can do for us. For centuries, people have been praying for God to save them, yet they continue to suffer as always. Those who have transcended suffering had to work hard.

As painful as it is to look at our life and feel the uncertainty and fear of losing what we have, it really is not a beneficial perspective, because it is very selfish. Let us all open our eyes. Instead of looking at the little log that we are clutching onto with so much attachment and fear, open your eyes and look around, and you will see that you are surrounded by millions upon millions of people in the same situation. This is what is truly terrifying, horrifying! If you are really sincere, you will burst into tears, because all of the people around you in the world are the people you have loved, and who have loved you. They are your mothers and fathers, your sons and daughters, your brothers and sisters, your wives and husbands. They are all suffering, and headed for more suffering. This is what true spirituality exists for: as a way to change that.

We put our situation into stark terms because that is our reality. We put it into stark terms not to encourage fear, nor to make us feel desperate, afraid, and worried, but because they are the facts, and we must see the facts in order to have a chance to change them.

It is not hard to see that the world is getting worse, and civilization is on the edge of complete failure. All the energy humanity has been putting in motion for centuries is cascading into a whirlpool of degeneration and pain.

Because of this, there are many people who give up on spirituality, because they become hypnotized by fear, shame, terror. They become overwhelmed; they defeat themselves; they feel, "It is too much for me; I can't handle it. It's too hard; I can't do it." Self-defeatism is a challenging opponent. Many use the words of spirituality to defeat themselves, saying that the state of the world demonstrates that God does not exist or does not care. All of this is due to grave misunderstandings of religion and scripture, and a profound lack of genuine knowledge.

What people do not realize is that in the midst of the greatest adversity is the greatest potential for positive change. The energy that is in motion can be a powerful catalyst for deep and lasting change.

What those who give up on spirituality need is to develop a genuine understanding of the law of karma. When you really understand the law of karma, then you will have great faith.

When you work seriously in your spiritual life, you will prove to yourself that it is possible to reach complete liberation. It can be done, but you have to invest energy into it. It cannot be a temporary or part-time job. It has to be full time.

Each little investment of energy we make results in a consequence that is greater than the energy invested. Each time that we meditate, each time that we restrain a harmful action and we turn it into something beneficial, we create a huge impact, not just for ourselves, but for others.

The Power of Generosity

The power of generosity is one of the greatest powers in the universe. The power of generosity is unimaginable. Generosity is the very basis of spiritual advancement: it is karma in motion, creating benefit. That is why all the great masters exemplify generosity—the power of sacrifice. In Kabbalah, that is the power of the sephirah Chokmah: love as sacrifice, the power of giving. It is a generosity of spirit, a generosity of heart.

True generosity is most accurately summarized as thinking of others before yourself. It is the most fundamental basis of real spirituality.

As we are now, we only think of ourselves, and when it is convenient to us, we might think of somebody else—only if it is convenient to us. That is not sacrifice. The true spirit of generosity is to constantly think of others first, especially in regard to our psychological work, our spiritual work. Some spiritual traditions talk about eliminating desire, but we usually think about eliminating desire in an egotistical way. We think, "I want to eliminate my egos so I can reach liberation (for myself)." It is very egotistical, and contradictory.

The opposite polarity of generosity is selfishness. The power of selfishness has created the state of the world today. All of the suffering of humanity is caused by selfishness.

All religions (before they become corrupted by selfishness) were originally conceived in order to guide us out of our selfish point of view, and learn how to become truly generous; that is, conscious of others. For this purpose, all religions were organized in levels, in order to prepare us to reach the heights of spiritual development. To reach very elevated levels requires a very powerful foundation. Imagine a tower. If the base is weak or easy to damage, the tower will fall. Similarly, we need a strong foundation. In spirituality, the foundation is a deep understanding of:

1. Impermanence

Death is inevitable. Our physical body is impermanent. Everyone "knows"

that, but few are they who really **know**
it. Those who comprehend that life is
impermanent and death certain do not
waste time on foolish activities. Moreover,
no matter how many possessions we accumulate during life, we do not take any of
it with us when we die. Those who comprehend this prefer not to waste so much
time and energy on material things.

2. Ethics

Every religion teaches ethics so that
we comprehend cause and effect (karma).
Every religion emphasizes that by doing
good deeds, we receive benefits. By
performing harmful actions, we receive
suffering.

At the foundational level of instruction, students are primarily concerned
with their own karma, their own suffering. In other words, while they may talk
about loving and serving others, their
actions are primarily driven by concern
for themselves. To advance to the next
level of instruction, that attitude has to be
transcended.

Selfish spirituality is not compatible with the higher trainings. To receive the higher teachings, you spontaneously have to be at that stage where you think of others first, where you start to realize: "I really need to eliminate my pride because it is hurting other people. I really need to eliminate my lust because it is hurting other people. This anger in me is hurting other people." When that is your first, spontaneous impulse, you are showing signs of being ready to enter into the middle level. In Buddhism, it is called Mahayana ("Greater Vehicle"). Jesus gave profound teachings about this level of instruction.

In order for us to enter the higher aspects of the path, such as the middle range of the path which is the Mahayana aspect, and then the Bodhisattva path, which is the Tantric aspect, we have to have a strong foundation first, which is the Sutrayana or foundational path. To have that foundation, we need to comprehend two primary aspects: death and Karma (cause and effect). None of us comprehend either. This is proven and easy to see. When we analyze just a day of our lives—yesterday, for example—if we are sincere with ourselves, we can see how much time we wasted in futility, in activities that are completely pointless, spiritually speaking, and the rest was spent thinking about ourselves. There is so much that we have been doing, spending time on, thinking about, being worried about, investing energy into, that are fruitless spiritually. Moreover, we do them thinking that we still have time on this planet, that we will not die. We believe that death may happen to everyone else but not us. We act in ways in which we think we will not bear the consequences, as if we can act, think, feel, and do what we like without receiving consequences. So, for example, we think lustful thoughts, we look lustfully at others, we nurse our anger, we feed our pride, we indulge in envy. All of these are done in ignorance of death and Karma. It is quite simple and quite sad, but these are the fundamental aspects. How can we expect to move on to the greater and higher aspects if we do not even grasp this today in our daily life?

As it is now, our mind is selfish. Even when the mind does charity and is gener-ous, it is always, in the end, acting for itself. We give donations and we do volunteer work, and on the outside we look like we are great saints and helping humanity, but really we are fattening up our pride. That is not real generosity. True generosity does not concern itself with itself. True generosity is love as sacrifice, giving because it must be given, at any cost—that is generosity, that is true compassion.

The highest level of spiritual instruction is given to those who embody generosity, and whose every action is done to benefit others. All of our greatest spiritual heroes attained this level of generosity, and sacrificed everything in order to help us realize how to stop suffering. That is why the beginning level of every religion is ethics: how to stop causing harm.

Stop Harmful Actions

The first, most important way for us to act for the benefit of self and others is to stop performing harmful actions. That means harmful actions towards ourselves or other people.

To understand what harmful actions are, we have to study the teachings; we have to study our religion. You can start by studying any religion to grasp this concept. This is the fundamental basis of any religion. It is the level where we learn ethics—what we should do, what we should not do. In general, the steps are pretty simple: do not kill, do not steal, do not lie, do not abuse your sexual energy, eliminate pride, eliminate anger, stop your selfishness. In general, it is to treat others as we would be treated. Of course, we all "know" this, but we do not do it, especially inside, in our minds and hearts.

In the western traditions are the Ten Commandments and other guides to a higher way of behaving. In the eastern traditions are the Vinaya, Pratimoksha, and many more presentations of ethics. There are many lists and analyses of the different actions that are harmful or beneficial. You can study any of those, and they will all help.

Most importantly, you have to study your heart. The truest guide for action is our own conscience. But to be guided by it, we have to learn to hear it.

We all have our own idiosyncrasies. We all have qualities that we think are virtues, that we think are our good qualities, which are actually completely egotistical, and no book is going to teach you that. You will only see that in yourself, in action, in your daily life. If you take this teaching seriously, you will see it, you will learn about it, because your Innermost Divine will show you.

The Innermost is our connection to the Divine. The Innermost is our Real Being. Our Being is divine, pure, eternal. It is our Spirit. It is not the Soul. It is not the mind or consciousness. The Innermost is our Inner Buddha or Angel, who waits to instruct us.

Whether we are spiritual or not, we experience situations in life that are painful, that are hard, partly because we created the conditions for them to arise, and also because our Innermost is putting us there to teach us about ourselves. When a puppy dog releases its wastes in the wrong place, in order to teach it we put its nose there and say, "Don't go here." Our Innermost Being does that with us, too. Our Innermost puts us into situations that we made, and says, "You made this mess. Do not do that. See how unpleasant it is? See how painful it is?" But we always curse God for our circumstances. We blame everything on others. We are unwilling to see ourselves. So we always say to ourselves, "Why is this always happening to me? Why do I have to suffer? Why these problems?" We do not realize that we made our life through our actions. We do not want to see our own culpability.

To be a serious spiritual practitioner, that is the first thing you look for in any situation: "How did I make this? How did I get myself in this position? What in me is suffering?" That is the best question of all. Instead of looking outside—"He is making me suffer; work is making me suffer; my wife is making me suffer"—look back at yourself and say, "What in me is suffering?" Because really, it is not your spouse that is making you suffer. It is your anger that is making you suffer; it is your pride that is making you suffer. If you did not have that pride, if you did not have that anger, their words would not have meant anything; they would not have affected you. Their actions would not have bothered you. But because you have pride and envy and anger, you get bothered a lot.

We have to stop harmful action, to restrain ourselves from any act of negativity. This alone can take many, many years. I know a lot of people like to think as soon as they enter into a religion and they read the list of commandments or vows, "Number one, two, three, four, five. Okay. I can do all these. I don't drink. I don't smoke. I don't sleep around. So I must be on my way to heaven." It does not work like that. Even though you may not be doing something physically, you are probably doing it in your mind. That is the hardest part. Jesus said,

> "Even if you look at a woman with lust, you have committed adultery."

In the state we are in, we constantly perform harmful actions in our body, feelings, and thoughts. In other words, we produce causes that create harmful effects, continually, because our desires are acting in us. So as part of this accurate analysis, we have to continually watch our behaviors and stop ourselves from doing harmful things, not just physically, but in the mind, in the heart, through our words, through our thoughts. This requires continual observation.

Self-observation is absolutely essential, critical—not just for a few minutes, but all the time. Never stop paying attention to your psychology. Do not get sucked into daydreaming, into being distracted by the outside world, by fantasizing on the inside world. Watch your mind, because at any instant, something in you is contemplating a harmful desire.

Samael Aun Weor said that ninety-seven percent of our thoughts are harmful and negative. If we are honest, how much do we really watch our mind during the day? Very little. What about all those other thoughts and feelings that have been surging throughout the day that we did not pay attention to? Those are all streams of energy that are creating effects. That should scare us into acting. That should be of great concern to us.

The instant we realize we have lost mindfulness of our actions, we should feel as if we have just discovered a serpent in our lap. We should be that astonished. Because truly, to lose attention is a life or death matter. When we cease paying attention, when we lose our cognizant awareness of the moment, we slip into sleep, and then all those psychological stimuli that are processing in our subconscious, unconscious, and infraconscious levels are creating effects. That is why life is getting more complicated and painful. That is why our society is declining: because nobody is paying attention to themselves.

Instead of being cognizant of ourselves, we act mechanically, we react and respond automatically, without consciousness of how or why. We are always dreaming about what someone meant, and what they "really" said. We project all kinds of interpretations of our daily lives. "When he looked at me like that, he must

have felt that I was doing something bad."
"When he looked at me like that, he must
have been lusting after me, so maybe he
likes me." We project so much garbage,
continually, replaying events and scenes
in our minds, trying to interpret them,
trying to analyze them, trying to change
them. It is all garbage, and we let it happen, and it has consequences. That is why
we are asleep. To awaken is to watch that,
to stop that, to be here and now, to be in
conscious dominion of our kingdom, to
control our mind, to be awake. That is
the prerequisite. We have to stop harmful
action, not just physically, but psychologically.

In many religions, this step is symbolized by death, such as in the beheading
of John, or the martyrdom of the saints.
Our desires must die in order for our
true potential to be born. If the seed does
not die, the tree cannot be born. Yet, if
the harmful action is restrained, then a
beneficial action can emerge. A beneficial
action—whether inside or outside—has
incredible power.

The Divine Virtues

Develop Virtue

The second step is to develop full and perfect virtue.

There are many ways of studying virtue in each tradition, and there are a lot of similarities among them: patience, tolerance, conscious love, humility, chastity, charity.

What does it mean to develop full and perfect virtue? It is not just to have a concept. It is not just to respect virtues, to say, "I have heard patience is a virtue, and I respect that, but get out of my way. I am in a hurry." To really develop full and perfect virtue is to be it, to actualize it. This is not to force it on yourself; it is not to force yourself into a rigid behavior because you "have to do it." It is to do it spontaneously, without force, because you realize you need to, that it is important, that it is beneficial for you and for others. True virtue is natural and spontaneous. It cannot be imitated, faked, or forced.

If you are angry with someone, and they are angry with you, and you are thinking "I have to be loving and forgiving," and you go to them and say resentfully, "Humph. I forgive you." That does not work; that is not honest. It is good as an action, and it does take courage. But it is far less powerful than a sincere apology. You can only be sincere when you have understood that your anger was wrong.

By understanding how an action creates suffering, we also can understand how an action can create happiness. Yet for happiness to emerge, the cause of suffering has to be removed; otherwise, it will remain a threat.

Liberation from suffering has three stages. The first stage is comprehension. The second stage is judgment. The third stage is elimination.

Many spiritual people love to talk about the elimination of desires or ego, and they love to do different practices to eliminate their egos. But rarely do you hear them talk about judgment and comprehension, which have to happen first, before you can reach elimination. You cannot eliminate something that still has your consciousness trapped in it; comprehension must come first. Nagarjuna, in

the following quotation, is talking about
this.

> "A wise person is one who has accu-
> rately analyzed all their actions and
> always acts for the benefit of self
> and others."

Comprehension comes from analysis
of oneself. Studying the scriptures, studying religion, is very important because it
gives us a foundation, but comprehension, wisdom, comes from inside. That
is why the Oracle of Delphi said, "Man,
know thyself." This is the prerequisite.
This is Gnosis: self-knowledge.

Self-knowledge is comprehension.
Comprehension is knowledge in the heart.

Comprehension is not found by making a list of your defects. It would be great
if spiritual advancement were that easy.
It might take us a while to write them all
down, but that is not comprehension.

Comprehension does not emerge
from reading books, theories, or beliefs.

Comprehension is very simple: it is
when you know something, not in your
intellect, but in your heart—when you
truly know it. If you have ever said some-

thing and seen the person who heard it react with pain, and then you felt pain and regret for saying it, that is comprehension. If you have ever given a gift, and saw how much gratitude that person had who received it, and you felt in your heart so much gratitude for the opportunity to give, that is comprehension.

Comprehension is not intellectual; it is emotional; it is intuitive; it is in your heart. Comprehension is not something that you develop by making lists and by making complicated explanations like, "Pride has this and that aspect, and these attributes, and it can manifest here and here." That is fine; we need to understand it in the intellect, but that is not comprehension.

When you have understood that an action is harmful and you have stopped it, you can then act virtuously, for the benefit of yourself and others. This type of action is the origin of all happiness in the world.

The development of virtue occurs naturally through comprehension of our actions and their effects. When you stop letting your anger control your mind, love naturally begins to emerge. Love for others is a source of immense happiness for everyone.

When we comprehend how our defects harm ourselves and others, we will spontaneously seek to act in ways that benefit others and give them happiness.

What is Happiness?

Society has many definitions for happiness, but none of them are genuine. We believe we are happy when we get what we desire, but that happiness quickly fades and a new desire emerges.

Real happiness is a state of consciousness and is not dependent upon external circumstances. That is, possessions are not the cause of happiness. All possessions are subject to loss, decay, and theft; they are impermanent and therefore unreliable.

Friends, acclaim, popularity, power, and all of the goals of this modern age do not bring happiness, because all of them are impermanent and unreliable. We take none of them when we die, and we will die.

For happiness to be genuine, it should not be dependent upon an unreliable foundation. Modern society believes that happiness is produced when we wear the latest fashion, drive the newest car, have the highest paying job, or we are feeding whichever desire happens to be strongest in us. Yet, this point of view is not only unrealistic, it is foolish. Genuine happiness can never be found through dependence upon unreliable, impermanent objects, people, or sensations. Nothing external can provide lasting happiness, thus the happiness they provide is shallow, brief, and ultimately unsatisfying. That is why we are continually dissatisfied, moving from one fascination to another, seeking a source of lasting happiness, but never finding it. The source of true happiness is within us.

Inside of us is something eternal, that never dies, and is the very root of our existence. It is a state of joyfulness and love, bright with contentment and deep, inner satisfaction. Unfortunately, we do not know how to experience this part of ourselves, because we have become so deeply fascinated with our desires and fears. Yet through training, we can abandon the illusions that cause us to suffer, and instead get to know the source of true happiness and fulfillment.

Observe a happy child. A truly happy child is happy just being. Even an impoverished, malnourished child can radiate joy. Personal experience in the presence of a child like this demonstrates to us the reality of genuine happiness and its fruit.

> "Except ye be converted, and become as [pure as] little children, ye shall not enter into the kingdom of heaven." - Jesus, from Matthew 18:3

Genuine happiness is a powerful catalyst. Like a sincere smile, genuine happiness spreads to others. This is a superior type of action that creates immeasurable benefit for everyone. Thus, acquiring genuine happiness for ourselves also benefits everyone we contact. A good example of the power of happiness can be observed in the 14th Dalai Lama. His presence affects everyone who meets him, even if they disagree with his religion or politics. His consciousness, being awake and happy, radiates those qualities effortlessly, inspiring others to become like him.

Our natural, original state of consciousness is pure happiness. By freeing ourselves of afflictive psychological conditioning—which is entirely within us, not outside—the natural state of our consciousness is restored. Then we experience genuine happiness. This is our birthright, but we have to work hard to restore it.

What is Suffering?

In the context of Gnosis, the word suffering is far more broad in its implications than mere physical, emotional, or mental pain. These are undoubtedly difficult and lamentable, but are mere side effects of the true cause. All suffering is rooted in a fundamental ignorance of our true nature.

In simple terms, suffering is any state of being that lacks contact with our inner source of serenity and happiness. There are many names for that source, but all point toward the same fundamental element: the consciousness, unobscured and free of the limitations imposed by desires, fears, resentments, and any type of cage.

In addition to the physical, emotional, or mental forms of suffering, a being is suffering when it lacks direct perception of its divine source—God, Allah, Buddha, or whatever name you want to use. This means that all of us are suffering. We might believe or disbelieve in God, we might imagine God, but that is not the same as seeing the Divine, talking to the

Divine, and getting answers and guidance from the Divine. Being united with the Divine is our natural state. When connected to our true nature, we are naturally content and happy. When we lack that connection, we are dissatisfied and anxious, always seeking something to fill the hole we feel inside. Unfortunately, this causes us to make a lot of mistakes.

Thus, we can see that suffering is not natural: it is the effect of a cause. The cause of suffering is the separation of the consciousness from its natural state. The natural state of our consciousness is a state of perfect happiness, joy, and freedom.

In Buddhism, the term nirvana refers to a state of cessation of suffering. That is, the consciousness has recovered its original state: union with the divine. In Sanskrit, this is called yoga, which means "to unite," and is synonymous with the Latin term religare ("to bind"), the root of the word "religion." Stated simply, until we are merged with our divine source, we are suffering. Only in "nirvana," or "heaven," do we experience a state of cessation of suffering. Nirvana, heaven, is a state of consciousness. It is also a place (or more accurately, places), but that correspond directly to states of consciousness. To enter those places, your consciousness has to vibrate at the same level.

As long as we do not have Gnosis—conscious knowledge—of the Divine, we are suffering. To be free of suffering, we have to restore our consciousness to its natural state. That is, we have to awaken, and stop acting in harmful ways.

How Suffering is Created

Suffering is created through action. Every form of suffering in existence has its root in an action performed by the one who is suffering.

The Four Ways to Create Suffering:

1. Harmful Actions:

    Against others (For example, gossip, killing, stealing)

    Against ourselves (For example, suicide, addiction, self-loathing)

2. Harmful Words:

    Against others (Speaking badly about others)

    Against ourselves (Speaking badly about oneself)

3. Harmful Thoughts:

    Against others (Wishing someone else will suffer)

    Against ourselves (Wishing we will suffer, as in an accident or with death)

4. Failing to act when we could.

> We acquire karma for the good
> deeds in word, action, or thought
> that we could perform, but do not.

Because we are mere beginners in this
type of training, our insight into how
these actions create results will be limited.
To really understand the whole scene of
life takes many years of effort and conscious development.

For the moment, because our situation—worldwide and as individuals—is so
complicated, we can rely on the insight of
those who have much deeper understanding than we do. Thus, here are some general indications of the results of mistaken
actions. These lines are quoted from
the Buddhist scriptures *Lam rim chenmo,
Satyaka-parivatara*, and *Dasabhumika-sutra.*

> "For the past act of killing, [you
> will have] a short lifetime, many ill-
> nesses.

> "For the act of stealing, [you will
> have] a lack of resources, poverty,
> or to have to share everything with
> others.

> "For sexual misconduct, [you will
> have] an untrustworthy spouse
> [adultery].

"For lying, your life will be filled with slander towards you, gossip about you and you will be deceived by others.

"For the past action of divisive speech, you will suffer loss of friend-ships and people you depend on will always be splitting and divisive with each other, so you cannot depend on them.

"For the past action of offensive speech, you will always hear unpleas-ant words and be surrounded by quarrels and arguments.

"For the past act of senseless speech, others will not listen to you, will not respect your words, will not under-stand your words, or you will have poor confidence in your words.

"For the past act of covetousness, you will suffer from attachment and have no contentment.

"For the past act of malice, others will be hostile towards you, and you will always be seeking things that are unbeneficial for yourself, always inadvertently harming others or being harmed by others.

Empty lot strewn with trash at 108th street and lexington avenue, manhattan. Photograph by gary miller

"For the past action of wrong views, you will suffer from confusion and deceit. Environmental effects are more widespread and in your environment.

"For the act of killing, you will have poor or little food, poor or ineffective medicine and the harvests and other resources that you bring will have little strength or will even produce illness.

"For the past act of stealing, you will also have poor crops, poor food, droughts, floods, spoiled foods, poisoned foods.

[...]

"For the past crime of sexual misconduct, you will live in filthy places, there will be excrement, urine, mud, vomit everywhere on the streets. You will have unclean things, bad smells, misery and discomfort everywhere.

"For the past crime of lying, your work does not flourish, there is no harmony in workers, everyone is deceitful, you will be fearful and have many causes to be afraid.

"For the past act of divisive speech, you will live in a place that is difficult to get around, and have many causes to fear.

"For offensive speech, you will live in a dangerous environment and no comforts such as parks or pools or safe places.

"For the past act of covetousness, all good things diminish every year and do not increase.

"For malice, you will be surrounded by epidemics, injury, infectious diseases, quarrels, disputes, harmful animals, thieves.

"For wrong views, the most important resources will be unavailable or too expensive, unclean things are plentiful, misery appears to be bliss, you will have no home, no protector and no refuge."

Who is the Cause of Suffering?

In us, by far the majority of our thinking is self-concerned. Most, if not all thoughts, are about ourselves and what we want. Most if not all thoughts are coming from selfish desire, from concern about "myself, me, what I want." It appears that we cannot control this tendency. Even when we seem to be doing something for someone else, our own interests still come first.

The outcome of our self-interest is actually quite logical: if everyone is thinking only about themselves, the result will be strife, disagreement, fighting, and inequality. When people think only about their self-interests, then violence will reign, and the strong will take from the weak. Is this not the state of our world? This may be what we consider "normal," but we only think it is normal because we have forgotten what normal really is. We have grown accustomed to our cage of suffering. The truth is that our society has been made by choice. It does not have to be as it is.

Science, which has long assumed that selfishness and violence are "human nature," has recently begun to question this position, based on evidence that the real basis of human nature is altruism: generosity, non-selfishness. Science is beginning to review evidence that violence and selfish behavior arise due to causes and conditions in our lives, and are not "normal" in our psyche. This agrees with all religions, which for centuries have said exactly that.

In fact, the true nature of all free, unconditioned consciousness is a profound awareness and sensitivity to the needs of others. This is why all true religions depend upon the foundation of love.

> "And one of the scribes came, and having heard them reasoning together, and perceiving that he had answered them well, asked him, 'Which is the first commandment of all?'

> "And Jesus answered him, 'The first of all the commandments [is], Hear,

O Israel; The Lord our God is one Lord: And thou shalt love the Lord thy God with all thy heart, and with all thy soul, and with all thy mind, and with all thy strength: this [is] the first commandment. And the second [is] like, [namely] this, Thou shalt love thy neighbour as thyself. There is none other commandment greater than these.'" - Mark 12

Through union with our true nature—which is a vibrant, bright, selfless love—we also unite with God (or Allah, Buddha, or whichever name you prefer), who is, in essence, cognizant love for all beings.

What does this have to do with cause and effect? It is simple:

> "All whosoever who are happy in the world
>
> "Are (so) through the wish for the happiness of others;
>
> "While all whosoever who are miserable in the world
>
> "Are (so) through the wish for the happiness of themselves." - Shantideva, Bodhicharyavatara

Selfishness is the devil itself, and the cause of all suffering. Conscious love—generosity—is the cause of freedom from suffering.

Many of us may think that karma only applies to actions like stealing or murder. But really, cause and effect applies to everything in life. Remember the words of the Master Jesus, when he said:

> "You have heard that it was said to the men of old, 'You shall not kill; and whoever kills shall be liable to judgement.' But I say to you that every one who is angry with his brother shall be liable to judgement; whoever insults his brother shall be liable to the council, and whoever says, 'You fool!' shall be liable to the hell of fire." - Matthew 5:21

Jesus gave us a tremendous clue in this wisdom, that we should understand the law with our conscience, and know that we can kill with a word, a glance, with our will. We can kill without a knife or a gun. He told us that even these actions, that seem so normal, so acceptable, are cause for judgement and punishment. He said what all spiritual traditions said: that we will reap only what we sow in life. As we do, so shall we receive.

If you continue day after day nursing resentments against your spouse, your coworkers, and continue feeding your anger toward your father and mother, and continue generating anger toward people on the street, in the grocery store, on the freeway, what do you think you are sowing in the field of your life? If you plant seeds of anger in the fields of your life, then happiness will not grow there. It is impossible. Yet, you expect happiness to come, no matter what you do.

Once we deeply comprehend this fact, we can see that we are responsible for the state of our life, we are responsible for the well-being of others, we are responsible for everything that we experience in life. Those who do not comprehend cause and effect blame others, and never recognize that the primary person who is at fault for our problems is OURSELVES. We are the cause of suffering.

> "Whatever affliction may visit you is for what your own hands have earned." - Qur'an 42.30

We all say, "If I had a better job" or a better husband or a better car or, "if I get this new computer or this new book or if I can make a little more money or move to a different city, then will I finally be contented and happy and then I will start to do good for others. I'll do some charity once I have everything I need."

We all say, "My boss is making me miserable, my sister is making me angry, my wife is making me anxious, my friend is making me jealous… and if they change, then things will be better for me. If my husband changes, then I can be a cheerful person. But as long as he keeps being the way he is, then I can't do it."

We create these illusions because we do not want to face the fact that our suffering is created by our own hands.

It is not my employer's fault if I am miserable at work. It is my reaction to work that creates my suffering. If I change my reaction or attitude, my experience at work can be totally different.

When we are suffering, it is our responsibility to see what in us is suffering, and how we created the circumstances for that suffering. Furthermore, we have to see how we have made others suffer in the same way.

Confucius said:

> "In vain have I looked for a single man capable of seeing his own faults and bringing the charge home against himself."

The one adopts this attitude no longer seeks blame outside, and instead, takes charge of their experience of life. They choose how to handle life. Would it not be better to choose how to respond to life?

> "Whatever harm a foe may do to a foe, or a hater to a hater, an ill-directed mind can do one far greater harm." - The Buddha Shakyamuni, from the Dhammapada, 42

Our habits of thinking, habits of feeling, and habits of action are all self-centered. None of us have selfless habits. This is a tremendous clue to us, a way for us to determine when and where we are acting in an out-of-balance way: we must begin to recognize when we are acting out of self-will. That is, seeking to satisfy ourselves, our sense of "me," our attachments, our desires, our wishes, our rules, our requirements, our demands, our dreams, our passions.

When we are concerned only with ourselves, or our own interests, who are we stealing from to do it? Who are we hurting in order to serve ourselves? What imbalances are we creating?

Observe the state of the world, the imbalances from culture to culture, and observe this in our city, in our families... It is quite evident that the state of our world is a result of this habitual fascination with "me, myself and I"...

When the rich hoard wealth and possessions, they are stealing it from their community. This creates imbalance, poverty, resentment, and violence. The end result is suffering for everyone. Every civilization has passed through upheavals caused by the disequilibrium of power and wealth. This will continue so long as one has, and another does not. Those who have should empower and nourish their neighbors. In this way, everyone benefits.

Suffering begins the moment we act from self-will. Remember the story of Adam and Eve: mankind was cast out of perfection when we acted from desire, and went against the law. Thus, we began to pay for our actions. Previous to that, we were in balance.

It is urgent for us to recognize our responsibility for our life. Everything in our lives is ultimately our responsibility, whether we like it or not. The sooner we recognize our responsibilities, the sooner we can change our life. It is only by recognizing that we create our own lives that we can begin to create a better one.

Those who continually blame others will remain victims of suffering. They will never stop suffering.

To escape suffering, one has to stop producing the causes of suffering.

> "I have heard and realized that bondage and salvation are both within yourself." - Acarangasutra 5.36

Karma is the Way to Liberation

If someone thinks well of you, this creates an impact on you. The thoughts and feelings of that person have consequences.

If someone screams in anger at you, it will have an undeniable effect on you. Even if someone feels anger toward you, you will sense it. Even if someone thinks angry thoughts about you, it will affect you.

Each stage—from intention, to feeling, to action—affects the angry one as well as the object of the anger. Anger is a handleless sword; it cuts the one who holds it. This is so because everything we feel, think, and do is energy.

Consider this: it is known in contemporary science that everything we see is an illusion. Mass is not really solid, nor is it lasting. All mass becomes energy and all energy becomes mass. This is something that was understood long before our scientists "discovered" it, of course, but even now it is something that none of us can really grasp.

At the bottom is this fact: everything in the universe is energy. Energy is manifest as vibration, and is characterized by constant transformation and change. Nothing is still or stagnant: everything is moving and changing.

We ourselves are undergoing constant transformation, though we are ignorant of it. Our bodies change dramatically every day, but we do not have the capacity to observe it.

Our bodies, our minds, our feelings, our thoughts, our dreams, our desires, our intentions, our wishes, everything is energy. A thought is energy. A feeling of love is an energy.

Wherever we are at this moment, there is a tremendous exchange of energy happening moment to moment. There are powerful atomic processes happening all the time, but we do not have the capacity to observe it.

As someone speaks to you they are sending energy to you. As you receive it there is a transformation that occurs in your psyche, in your mind, and hopefully, if you are present and aware and not daydreaming, there is a transformation in your consciousness.

Likewise, as you think and feel there are energies that are being processed: all of this exchange of energy is a process of creation and destruction.

In all transformation, there is birth and there is death.

When you think, something is created.

When you feel, something is created.

Karma is not limited to mere physical action. It concerns the entirety of life, from the first moment to the last. Every moment is a moment in which something is created. In every moment, something is destroyed.

When you eat, you destroy mineral, plant, and animal life. When you eat, you create life: your own, and all those you support in turn. Therefore, even eating is karma: cause and effect, in which death and life are balanced.

The law of karma is the law of the balance. Science calls this Invariance. That is all karma is: the natural function of nature to balance energy. Karma is not a law of punishment or vengeance, nor is it merciless. In fact, as you will see later in the book, the existence of karma is a sign of the compassion of the Divine.

Just as your actions have created effects, so too then you can act in different ways, to create different effects, and cancel your debts. You can work with the law, to be in accordance with the law, in harmony.

The lion of the law is combated with the scale. If you want to conquer the suffering in your life, you need to tip the scale in your favor.

How to Stop Suffering

If karma did not exist, there would be no free will. Yet, if there were no consequences for our actions, all of us would be forever enslaved by the tyranny of a powerful oppressor who never had to answer for his crimes. Fortunately, cause and effect does exist, and every action bears a consequence for its originator. Furthermore, once the consequence is complete, the debt is paid. No suffering lasts forever.

The law of karma is not "out to get you." Law without mercy is tyranny, and the Divine is not cruel and unjust. The Divine is pure love and wisdom. How could the Divine wish you to be eternally in suffering? Hell, suffering, exists as long as there are debts to be paid. When the debt is paid, the suffering ends.

Therefore, no matter your situation or how grave your suffering, there is a way to resolve it. The power to change our karma begins within us.

Every religion in the world began by instructing its students in ethics, not morality. Nowadays most religious systems have become mere morality or philosophy. Yet true ethics are not "morals."

Morals change with time and with culture. Behaviors that are moral in North America are immoral in Asia. Behaviors that are moral in Asia are immoral in the west. Thus, morality is subjective. Morality is not eternal, immutable, and infallible. Morality changes with time and culture.

Ethics, on the other hand, are eternal. True ethics—conscious ethics—are laws of nature. Religions originally emerged from cognizant knowledge of those ethical laws, even if later the religions degenerated and collapsed into moral dogmas.

In Judeo-Christian traditions, ethics were synthesized in the Decalogue, the Ten Commandments. These are ethics formulated as "Thou shalt not kill," "Thou shalt not covet," "Thou shalt not commit adultery, fornication," "Thou shalt honor thy father and mother," etc. All of the commandments have an ethical foundation. The Ten Commandments are not the only representation of ethics in the Jewish or Christian traditions, they are just a simplified synthesis of them.

In Hinduism there are many presentations of ethics. Probably the most famous is in Patanjali's Yoga Sutras, which is an exposition of Raja Yoga. The first two steps of Raja Yoga are Yama and Niyama, which are ethics and observances, and refer to what you should do and what you should not do.

Buddhism, Islam, and every other spiritual tradition present a wide range of ethical instruction, but unfortunately, nowadays people ignore the ethical guidelines, or merely respect them but do not attempt to apply them, or they interpret the instructions very literally, and allow themselves lots of loopholes, especially among the so-called elite, such as priests and students of esoteric instructions, who believe they have transcended the "basic" stages of their traditions. This is why we can find so much mistaken behavior in followers of every religion, even to the point that people kill, rape, steal, and lie, all the while claiming to be "religious."

In general, followers of religions lack understanding of why ethics are important.

Ethics are not just mechanical laws that some external authority is trying to impose upon us. The ethical rules, commandments, or vows have a very specific function, which must be clearly grasped, and that is this: If you perform actions that are harmful, you create disharmony not only in your environment but in your mind.

Someone who steals creates disharmony in their mind. They become addicted to the excitement of the act. They become addicted to the fear of being caught. They lose respect for others and themselves. They cease to care about other people, and only see others as targets to steal from. They even begin to hate others, and want to steal in order to punish them. Thieves become liars to themselves and to others. All of this causes the mind to be disturbed.

The same happens with all actions that contradict ethical behavior.

Yet if you follow the "observances," or positive behaviors, you create positive energy, not only into your environment, but in your mind. The purpose of Raja Yoga's stages of Yama and Niyama or the Commandments of Moses is to stabilize our psyche so that we are no longer vibrating with so much negative emotion. For example, any Buddhist, whether a lay person or an ordained monk, always takes five fundamental vows:

- to not steal
- to not kill
- to not lie
- to not commit sexual crime
- to take no intoxicants

Each of these actions creates a great energetic disturbance in the mind and environment. These types of energetic disturbances prevent quietude and peace of mind. They disturb the consciousness, and trap it in harmful qualities. In such psychological circumstances, it becomes impossible to experience your true nature, the free consciousness. Consciousness intoxicated with alcohol or drugs can only perceive through the influence of those chemicals, thus it cannot see reality clearly. Someone who lies is influenced

by the energetic consequences of the lie,
they obscure the truth from others, and
cannot see the truth themselves. Each of
these actions creates powerful energetic
disturbances.

If you observe yourself, you can see
how true this is. When a strong negative
emotion like anger or lust takes a hold
of you, you cannot relax, you do not have
a calm mind; you are very agitated. That
agitation is precisely what prevents us
from seeing the truth. When we are very
angry, we only see through that anger.
Everything we perceive is changed by
that anger. We only want what that anger
wants. In a fit of anger, we can even throw
away a marriage, our job, or our social status. Anger is totally irrational and dangerous. That is what anger does to us: anger
makes us destroy, and in turn it destroys
us. So does every other negative quality:
lust, envy, gluttony, greed, fear, laziness,
etc. With conscious ethics, we are trying
to regulate these qualities, and eliminate
them.

> "Like a poison that has been ingest-
> ed, the commission of even a small

sin creates in your lives hereafter great fear and a terrible downfall.

"As when grain ripens into a bounty, even the creation of small merit [from virtuous action] leads in lives hereafter to great happiness and will be immensely meaningful as well." - Udana-varga (Collection of Indicative Verses)

A Buddhist scripture describes how the king of the Nagas came to the Buddha with questions, and the Buddha told him:

"Lord of Nagas, a single practice of the Bodhisattvas correctly stops rebirth in the lower realms. What is this single practice? It is the discernment of what is virtuous. You must think, 'Am I being true? How am I spending the day and the night?'" - Sagara-naga-raja-pariprccha (Questions of the Naga Kings of the Ocean)

That single perspective or point of view can take you all the way on the path to the full development of your true nature. Thus, from moment to moment you have to question yourself: "Am I being true?" To do this, you have to first be aware of yourself from moment to moment. Pose that question when you are tempted by lust, pride, or fear. "Am I being true?"

Who is that 'I', first of all? And secondly, what does it mean to be true? To whom? Are you true to your Divine Being, true to your Innermost, true to your Divine Mother and Father?

This questioning reveals to us that the beginning of our spiritual work and the ending of our spiritual work are the same: throughout our entire spiritual path we have to be inquiring into ourselves: "Am I being true? How am I spending the day and the night? What am I doing with my mind, with my body?" This question has to be ever present. However, if the question is to bear fruit, we need to have good understanding of these fundamental aspects of the path. We need to know how to answer the question, "Am I being true? Who am 'I'?" We have to be able to answer that. To answer it, we have to awaken from moment to moment, and change our behavior.

Ten Non-virtuous Actions

While every religion has a variety of ways of learning about harmful actions, here we will study a simple approach known in Buddhism.

Among his many other ways of teaching about this subject, the Buddha taught that there are ten non-virtuous actions. This does not mean that these ten non-virtuous actions are the only wrong actions. So for example, in this list of ten, he does not mention taking drugs, or drinking alcohol, or beating your children. These actions are still wrong, they are still harmful, they just do not happen to be in this list.

This list examines fundamental psychological axioms that we need to understand. The first three are considered to be actions of body. Buddhism tends to look at the potentials for Karma as emerging in three ways: physically, verbally, or mentally. Buddhism studies action of our:

· body

· speech

· mind

> "What is karma that you have done?
> An action that you have thought
> about or that you have set into
> motion either physically or vocally."
> - Yoga-carya-bhumi

These are three doorways through which we utilize energy. But again, do not think that these are the only ways to create Karma. This is just a model to help you get on your way towards analyzing yourself, but these do not include everything. As a matter of fact, these ten non-virtues are generally studied after somebody has already taken other vows, such as, do not kill, do not steal, do not lie, do not have sexual misconduct, do not take intoxicants, etc. So these ten non virtuous actions come after that.

Killing

In Buddhism, the first non virtuous act is called killing. We tend to interpret this as the act of murder, which of course, creates a lot of harm.

To kill a physical body is a grave crime. Yet, killing is not merely related to the physical body. We can kill with a word. We can kill with silence, because we can kill not merely the body, but the spirit. We can kill someone's mind. We can kill someone's heart.

To kill is to take someone's life, to take the life of another being. In the scriptures it is stated that this is a right reserved only for God. Depending upon the religion or tradition you study, that right may be further elaborated. For example, there are what we call angels of death, which are Devas or Buddhas who are responsible for ending the life of creatures. In this case, killing is not a crime, it is their job, their duty, and it is performed with love. Likewise, there are cosmic executioners whose job is to kill, as punishment, and as compassion.

In Kabbalah, killing is the domain of the sephirah Geburah (literally, "severity") in the Tree of Life. Each sephirah is a world, an energy, a psychological aspect, and much more. Geburah is the sephirah of justice, and it is ruled by the angel Samael. This is why the mystical scripture

The Zohar says that the powerful angel Samael is the angel of killing. The Angel Samael has the right to kill in accordance with karma, in accordance with the law. There are many great masters, great teachers, great illuminated prophets, who acquire this right. The great masters David, Solomon, Padmasambhava, Quetzalcoatl, and others—in accordance with the law of karma—were able to kill without accruing any debt. We are not at that level. We do not have that right. But, we think we do.

Most people think, "I have never killed anyone, so this does not apply to me." I am sorry, but it does. Our society is as it is because of who we are as individuals. All of us share in the karma of killing. Which civilization, which country on this planet is responsible for the most wars and killing? Which civilization, which country on this planet is spending the most money developing and perfecting the art of killing? The United States. The vast majority of the money that comes out of the United States is spent on the act and the art of killing. Why? There are a lot of "reasons," a lot of "justifications." Some may be good, some may be not. But it is an undeniable truth, and all of the citizens of the United States are participants in that killing, in some form, at some level, whether through active participation or through apathy, everyone contributes. None of us, in any part of the world, are innocent.

Many of us are being trained daily in the art of killing. Most television shows for the last few decades are about killing. Those who watch television are trained daily in how to murder. Media celebrates criminals, murderers, serial rapists, gangsters, war, and all of us indulge in these movies and TV shows, and think, "It is just entertainment" without realizing that information is going into the brain and is teaching us how to kill. Is this what we need to learn? What will be the consequences of a society that loves to watch death and killing, and the many "creative" ways there are to harm one another? Remember: cause and effect. If you teach generation after generation of children how to use weapons, how to handle guns, how to shoot, how to stab, what will be the result? Peace, serenity, a golden age? Or war and killing? No peace ever came from killing. Killing only creates more killing.

What about video games? Have you noticed that the most popular video games are always games about killing, with extreme violence? Our children are spending hours and hours teaching themselves how to kill: to enjoy it, to indulge in it. Again, there may not be a physical act, but there is a psychological environment that is being created.

If we wonder why there is so much violence in the United States and North America because of guns, the people who live there have to look to themselves for the cause. If we wonder why there is so much violence in the Middle-East and Africa because of guns, the people who live there have to look to themselves, not blame other countries, but look to themselves. The causes are within us.

We kill others with our sarcasm, which is a form of verbal violence.

We kill with our anger and resentment.

We kill with our greed, when we refuse to share our wealth or resources with others.

We kill with our silence, when we do not speak to protect the weak or suffering, or to point out crimes.

We kill spiritually when we prevent others from receiving the true teachings, or when we spread false teachings. There are millions of people with very good intentions who are killings souls right now, because they are spreading spiritual lies.

Our desires cause us to kill in many ways. If we become fully conscious of our actions and their effects, then we can stop harming others. But for this, we have to change our behaviors in a radical way.

Stealing

In regard to stealing we tend to think of a thief wearing a little black mask around his eyes who sneaks into a house at night to steal jewels. Yes, that is stealing, but that is relatively rare compared to the kind of stealing that we all do every day. It is a crime to steal energy, attention, ideas, the truth. We steal in many ways, not just by taking a possession. We may take away someone's identity. If you have ever had a dream that someone steals your driver's license, passport, or wallet, that means someone in the physical world is criticizing you, harming your image, taking away your identity, making you look bad. When we criticize, gossip, lie, point out defects of others, and otherwise calumniate or bring someone down, we are stealing their social image from them. This is wrong. Why do we do it? Because of our pride, resentment, and envy.

Samael Aun Weor wrote that the true spiritual aspirants are always surrounded by many people trying to destroy their image, accusing them of stealing money, of being a homosexual, a fornicator, an adulterer, a liar. Every spiritual aspirant, true spiritual aspirant faces this. Why does it happen? Because all the people in the spiritual community have envy, pride, fear, resentment. Those who spread gossip are stealing the reputations of others.

Deceit is a form of stealing. When you misrepresent something, you steal. What can we say about all these companies who make big promises and offer beautiful products for us to purchase, and then when we buy it, it is cheap junk, it does not work, or it breaks the day the warranty ends? This is deceit, it is stealing; it is wrong. How many companies or people out there genuinely want to make something that is really good and worth it and will last a long time?

Everybody is trying to get something for nothing. Nowadays, this is a big obsession: to get something for nothing, such as to win the lottery, which is, by the way, a form of deceit sanctioned by authority.

What can we say of people who are professional deceivers? Who are paid, who make their living by deceiving others? Some of us may be those people and we should carefully analyze what we do with our time. Many of us are paid to lie.

Sexual Misconduct

The third non-virtuous action—and we are still talking about actions primarily related with the body—is sexual misconduct. Sexual misconduct is a very vast topic, and the true importance of sex in spirituality has only recently been publicly revealed. The full teaching about upright sexuality can be found in books like *The Perfect Matrimony* and *The Mystery of the Golden Blossom* by Samael Aun Weor.

Sexuality is a necessary part of life. Sex is how life is created and sustained, and this is especially true in spiritual life.

Jesus said,

> "Verily, verily, I say unto thee, Except a man be born of water [sexual energy] and of the [Holy] Spirit, he cannot enter into the kingdom of God. That which is born of the flesh [through common sex] is flesh; and that which is born of the Spirit [through immaculate sexuality, as required in Leviticus 15] is spirit. Marvel not that I said unto thee, Ye must be born again [for everything that exists is born of sex, so must the soul be]." - Jesus, from John 3

Jesus taught sacred sexuality, but for two thousand years his teachings have been heavily edited.

Sexual misconduct is any misuse of sexual energy in our body, speech, or mind. Our modern society is constructed on sexual misuse.

Those who are serious about spiritual development have to convert their sexual power into a spiritual power. This can only be done when we understand and renounce sexual misconduct.

The most basic definition of sexual misconduct is fornication: the orgasm. To understand fornication, you have to study the secret teachings of any religion. No ordinary dictionary or exoteric teaching will explain the real meaning of fornication to you, because that aspect of the sacred teaching has been preserved in secret in order to keep it pure. Yet, there are hints in every scripture and religious text [visit sacred-sex.org].

> "A person's approach to sexuality is a sign of his level of evolution. Unevolved persons practice ordinary sexual intercourse. Placing all emphasis upon the sexual organs, they neglect the body's other organs and systems. Whatever physical energy is accumulated is summarily discharged [through orgasm], and the subtle energies are similarly dissipated and disordered. It is a great backward leap." - Hua Hu Ching 69 (Taoism)

> "When a man discharges semen, he must immerse his entire body

in a mikvah [ritual bath], and
[then] remain unclean until eve-
ning." - Leviticus 15:16 (Judaism /
Christianity)

"That which is called Brahmacharya
[transformation of sexual energy] is
regarded as the means of attaining
to Brahma [God]." - Mahabharata
(Hinduism)

"Flee fornication [orgasm]. Every
sin that a man doeth is without
the body; but he that committeth
fornication sinneth against his
own body." - 1 Corinthians 6
(Christianity)

Sexual purity is a state in which the
sexual energy is restrained, purified, and
redirected, whether as a married or a
single person. Sexual purity is a way of life
observed by Jesus, Buddha, Mohammed,
Moses, Krishna, Padmasambhava, and
every great master. The teachings of sexual purity have only been given to those
who have proven their ability to use it
properly, thus the public has never heard
of it. Instead, the public worships sexual
misconduct, and will fight to the death

to defend it, even though it is the primary cause of their suffering.

Sexual misconduct includes fornication, adultery, homosexuality, and masturbation.

Sexual misconduct includes trying to have sex with your spouse when they are ill or not interested or against their will or when they are pregnant or menstruating. Having the sexual act in sacred places is wrong. It is wrong to have sex with children, prostitutes, renunciates. There are many ways we commit harmful sexual actions.

Pornography is sexual misconduct because it is a form of adultery. Jesus said in the gospels that when you look at a person with lust, you have committed adultery with them in your heart, thus in doing so, you have broken a commandment. But Jesus was not the only one to say that; the Buddha said it also five hundred years before Jesus.

> "Commit no adultery. This law is broken by even looking at the wife of another with a lustful mind." - Buddha

It is also in the mystical Hebrew scripture *The Zohar.*

> "...it is prohibited for a man to look at the beauty of a woman to prevent him from acquiring bad thoughts and being torn into another thing [meaning semen will be torn from him and wasted]." - Zohar 33. Kedoshim:10

In every tradition, pornography, or looking at others lustfully, is defined as unethical. Sexual misconduct is not merely a physical act, it is in the mind and the heart.

Adultery is any act that corrupts something that was once pure. To adulterate means to change or corrupt something, to make it impure. We tend to think of adultery as just sex between a married person and someone else, another married person maybe. But no, not according to this doctrine, not according to any true religion. That is a form of adultery, yes, but not the fundamental form. The fundamental form occurs the instant we allow ourselves to have lust towards another person, even our spouse. Lust is a form of adultery; it brings impurity to the consciousness, it dirties the soul, it puts filth into the temple of God, which is within. Let us be clear however; this is not to condemn sex, because sex is natural and normal. Yet, it is only normal when that sex, that sexual act, that sexual emotion is illuminated with the presence of God, when it is pure.

The first three non-virtuous actions are related with the body. The next few are related with speech.

Lying

The fourth non-virtuous action is lying. To lie is possible even without speaking. We can lie with our silence, we can lie with a gesture, we can lie with a word. Moreover, we can cause others to lie, either for ourselves or to others when we affirm something that is not true.

What is the gravest form of lie? It is the spiritual lie. When we affirm something spiritual or religious that we do not know is true, we commit a horrible action whose Karma is extremely intense. For example: if we join a group, a spiritual movement, a religion, and we begin to preach and try to bring people into that religion but it is all a lie, whether we know it or not, we have accrued a very serious Karma. When you lie to the soul, you affect the inner Being of that person, you affect their spiritual development. This is an act equivalent to killing, because you kill the soul. For example: there are many groups and schools who are working very hard to spread degenerated spiritual teachings that encourage indulgence in desire, indulgence in lust, indulgence in the ego; they are committing a form of deceit of the most serious type, because they are affirming to the souls that follow them that desire and lust is okay with God. This is not true, and no authentic scripture in the world affirms it. This is an extremely serious crime whose consequences will reverberate far into the future, not merely with consequences in this lifetime, but in future lifetimes.

This is why it is such a serious step to become a spiritual teacher. If you have not experienced the results of a spiritual teaching, then you restrain yourself from spreading them until you do. Confirm the teachings completely, through experience. Then you can teach without fear, and teach with confidence. Too often we hear instructors repeating what others have said, or quoting from popular theories and beliefs, because they do not want to contradict what is popular or what people like. We have to teach the truth, but we first have to know what the truth is.

Divisive Speech

The next non-virtuous action is divisive speech. Divisive speech is related to actions in which we try to separate people from each other, or keep them separated. In some families, for example, there may be an argument and one sister will not talk to the other sister. If we get involved and say "You shouldn't talk to her, she's really bad, she shouldn't have done that." That is wrong. This behavior is very common in the workplace.

Some people love to split others into groups, to divide people, control them, and manipulate them. Usually, the people who do this appear quite innocent or as "martyrs" who seem to deserve our sympathy.

How can we be a spiritual person when we are trying to separate people from each other? Real spirituality is about bringing people together, cultivating harmony, mutual respect, tolerance, peace, not divisiveness and contention.

The gravest form of divisive speech is when it is performed in spiritual groups. In some scriptures, it is said that this is the worst crime of all crimes: worse than killing, worse than fornication, worse than adultery is the crime of divisive speech in the spiritual community. Some say it is worse than the crime of killing a Buddha, so it is very serious. Yet, everyone is doing it. Anytime someone is making statements like, "That group is no good, you should stay away from them. They are bad people. They are not true to the lineage. They are not true to the master. They are merchants in the temple. They have left the path. They are not serious. They are all black magicians." These are all forms of divisive speech and they are extremely serious problems. This is rampant in every spiritual tradition. Every group claims that their group is the only true and good group. It ridiculous to see all these different groups saying "We are the good ones, not them!" This is all lies. Let me tell you something: there are no good groups, not on this Earth. Do you want to find a good spiritual group? Then go to heaven: visit the internal worlds, bow at the feet of your inner Master, then you will find a good group. In the physical world, it is impossible to find a good spiritual group. All of us here have too much ego. All of us here are liars, cheats, adulterers, murderers, and fornicators, without exception. Everyone who says otherwise is a liar. These so-called leaders who claim to be illuminated ones or incarnations of "master so-and-so," they are all liars. The real master we need to follow is within. The real group we need is within.

Divisive speech is a major crime because it separates the Sangha, the spiritual community. It empowers the ego. When groups are divisive, split, and separated into many different small factions and not united, they are weak. How can they fight if they are weak? How can they work for humanity if they are all separated and fighting with each other because of politics, gossip, rumors, and pride? They cannot. This is a problem that Paul wrote about in the years after Jesus. It was a problem then, it is a problem now. Gossip, rumors, pride, divisive speech, all of this interrupts the efforts of the Divine to help us.

Offensive Speech

The sixth harmful action is offensive speech. Offensive speech encompasses a wide variety of actions. Speaking critically of others, condemning others, attacking others, even attacking ourselves can be offensive. When our hostility, malice, and anger are coming out through our words, whether written or spoken, or even in our silence, it is offensive speech.

I once visited a spiritual instructor's home with a group of other people and we were all having a very pleasant conversation, when suddenly the wife of the instructor came in the room and the whole tone of the room changed. When I looked at her, she did not say a word, but she was raging with anger. It affected everyone. It interrupted the entire purpose of our gathering. This was an example of offensive speech through silence. You see, she had a lot of resentment at some of the people that were gathered there and she was unwilling to transform it. I understand that and I feel bad that she made this mistake because it is going to affect her later if she does not deal with it.

Offensive speech is any means of communication that creates hostility or pain.

Senseless Speech

The seventh harmful action is senseless speech. We tend to think of "senseless" as words that have no meaning, but this action relates to speech that is senseless in terms of spirituality. For example, we spend hours talking about sitcoms or about celebrities, about our neighbors private lives, etc. That is senseless speech.

Any means of communication that has no spiritual value is senseless speech. You do not have to speak it, you can indulge in it mentally. Reading magazines is senseless speech. Television is senseless speech. Most of the internet is senseless spiritually and creates harm.

Talking about things that are a waste of time is senseless speech. Gossip is senseless speech. "Did you hear that story? Did you hear what such and such person did? I cannot believe it, is it true?"

Swami Sivananda has a very colorful phrase to describe this harmful action: "diarrhea of the tongue." Senseless speech is marked in those people who cannot control their tongue, who are always going on, "Blah blah blah blah blah blah blah," all day long. A person like that cannot meditate. That tongue is showing what their mind is doing. If you want to control your mind and have serenity of mind and enter into calm abiding, control your tongue. James said in the Bible:

> "...the tongue is a little member, and boasteth great things. Behold, how great a matter a little fire kindleth!
>
> "And the tongue [is] a fire, a world of iniquity: so is the tongue among our members, that it defileth the whole body, and setteth on fire the course of nature; and it is set on fire of hell." - James 3

If you want to know more about your tongue, study the Book of James in the New Testament. He gave a very beautiful, profound teaching about the tongue.

Talking about things that do not contribute to spirituality or our wellbeing is considered senseless speech. We need to talk a certain amount about our jobs, school, educating children, feeding ourselves, taking care of our lives. This is not senseless speech, these are important things that need to be talked about and discussed. Ethical speech does not mean that every time you open your mouth you have to talk about scripture. It means when you open your mouth, you talk consciously, and you know what you are saying and why you are saying it.

The remaining non-virtuous actions are related with the mind.

Covetousness

The eighth non-virtuous action is covetousness. Samael Aun Weor said that envy is the secret trigger of all action in the world. When we analyze what is happening with our governments, with big companies, with our family members, with ourselves, we can pretty much always find envy.

Envy is to want what someone else has. We want that car, we want that job, one country wants the resources of another, wants the respect of another, one family member wants the money of another, the love that another one gets. Envy is when we want something that is not naturally ours. Envy always says, "I want it. I deserve it."

Envy is common in relation with material things. "I want money, a spouse, a better place to live, a big house, an island." We have a list in our mind, probably since we were children. I will give you a little secret: Burn your list. You will have peace when you have no covetousness, when you are content with what the Divine has given you.

> "...as God hath distributed to every man, as the Lord hath called every one, so let him walk." - 1 Corinthians 7:17

We are all scratching out a living trying to get more and more and more. Why? Because we have not comprehended death. We have not understood that we are going to die and all of those things we are working so hard to get will be useless. Why spend years and years struggling so hard to get something that, in the end, we have to give up?

When a desire emerges in you, reflect: "What will this fundamentally change for my soul? What will this change about the moment I am dying?"

Have you meditated on the moment of your death? Sit and imagine it. Do not hide from it, do not run from it. If you avoid death, when it comes you will be unprepared, and you will die in a panic and afraid, and those energies will affect your transition. But if you prepare every day for death, it will not come as a surprise, you will be ready, and you will pass into that transition with happiness, contentment. The true spiritual aspirant prepares for death every day. The true spiritual path is a path of dying from moment to moment, preparing for death. If you are doing that, what is there to be attached to? Why do you really need more shoes or more pants or that new computer, or to redecorate the whole house? There is nothing is wrong with those objects, what is wrong is our attitude and our enslavement to attachment.

Attachment is the key factor of covetousness. The state of our world is because of this envy. Yes, we have killing, we have lying, we have deceit, we have divisive speech; we have all those things but the key to suffering on this planet is covetousness. No one is content with what they have, and they want what the neighbor has. Because of envy we kill our neighbor, we lie about our neighbor, we deceive our neighbor, we go to war.

Here are some examples that you can look for in your mind: "How nice if I were the one in charge." You might think, "That does not sound like covetousness to me, it sounds like pride." But it is covetousness. How else will we get the idea unless we are trying to get it from someone else? We see the boss who is in charge, "Look at that nice car he drives, everybody respects him, they bow at his feet when he walks by, everybody salutes the guy in charge, I want to be that guy." That is covetousness. This applies spiritually, too. A lot of people want to be the master who all the students bow to. Why? Not to benefit the students, but to get the praise, to feed pride, to hide from their fear.

"How nice to have the wife of so-and-so, to have their possessions? How nice if I could eat that food?" This is all covetousness.

"How nice if others knew me to be humble, to be compassionate, to be wise?" Every spiritually inclined person has thought that. "I hope everybody can see me as a spiritual person, very humble." That is covetousness. That is not true spirituality.

When you want something from someone else, when you are attached to how people see you, when you want their attention, when you want their respect, it is covetousness.

"How nice if people in high places respected me?" Some people think, "If everybody respected me, even celebrities would respect me, even politicians would respect me." That is covetousness.

"How nice if I could be reborn in Nirvana (heaven) with powers and servants." Covetousness.

"How nice if I had the ability to go in the astral body. How nice if I was a master of Samadhi." Covetousness.

We should not covet what we do not have. If you want something different, analyze that want, and give it to God. This does not mean that you sit back and wait. There is a great quote from the

Muslim tradition: "Pray to Allah but tie your camel to the post." There is another one I like even better, I do not know where it comes from: "Pray to catch the bus, but run like hell."

We have to give up our desires, analyze our wants, but we also have to work for what is right. Some people say, "If I accept what God has given me, does that mean I do not have to work? Does that mean I should quit my job? If I am not supposed to worry about my clothes and paying my bills and eating, should I just stop doing anything?" No, because if you do not do anything, you will starve. You have to work, you have to act, you have to be prudent, you have to be intelligent. But, you should accept what you are given, and curb your desires.

Malice

The ninth non-virtuous action is called harmful intent, or malice. This is any desire or any thought or action directed towards causing harm for others. Our anger wishes others to suffer. We imagine our enemies suffering. We imagine our boss getting fired. We imagine our spouse getting a divorce and being miserable because we left her or him. We imagine our parents suffering in loneliness because of our resentment to them. We imagine our friends missing us because we do not call them back. We imagine our coworkers confused because we do not speak with them. These are all malice; they are the intent to harm.

Any attitude of hostility is malice. It is very common now to find an attitude of hostility in people. How rare is it to find sincere kindness? How easy to find hostility?

Impatience with others is a form of hostility, malice. When we become impatient, we become angry, we want others to serve us, especially when we are hungry. Impatience is hostility. When you have that thought, imagining, "I wish that person would just go to hell." That is malice, that is harmful intent. Directing curse words at another, even just in the mind, is harmful intent. That is the opposite of compassion.

How interesting it is that we speak and think without cognizance of what we are saying. We say to people, "Go to hell."

Or we say "I'm going to kill you." "I could have killed her." We do not think about what is behind those words. The personality thinks, "It is just a phrase that we toss around nowadays, it does not mean anything." Then why do we say it? What is behind it? What psychological element is behind those phrases? We should analyze those tendencies.

Wrong Views

The tenth non-virtuous action is wrong views, ways of seeing life that keep us doing wrong things. In other words, until we awaken consciousness, our entire way of being is a series of wrong views.

Right view is a conscious perception of reality that sees not only the fundamental nature of existence, but also sees everything with profound compassion, kindness, wisdom, and intelligence. Right view is the way an angel or Buddha sees. To acquire that type of vision is only possible when every atom of impurity has been removed from us.

Primarily, for our perspective at this moment, wrong views include to be ignorant of the reality of death. To be ignorant of the reality of cause and effect. To be willfully ignorant of the reality of a higher life. Many of us willfully ignore these truths. Many people, when they encounter this type of teaching, cannot bear it. It stimulates too much pain in the heart, it stimulates too much doubt in the mind, too many conflicts, and so they prefer to ignore it. This is to willfully ignore something that is fundamentally true.

Wrong views include any attitude that delights in wrong action. Any attitude in us that indulges in lust, that delights in pride, that delights in gossip, that delights in killing, that delights in stealing; these are all wrong views.

Any attitude or point of view that fails to recognize the truth of our situation is a wrong view. When we fail to be conscious of the needs of others or ourselves, that is a wrong view. When we fail to remember the Divine from moment to moment, that is a wrong view.

Right view is a conscious perception of reality.

CHARITY BY GIOTTO DI BONDONE

Ten Virtuous Actions

Each of the ten examples of non-virtuous actions provided by the Buddha are motivated by selfishness, and perpetuated by a lack of cognizant knowledge. When we are infected by a desire, we do not want to know that our actions are harmful; we are only interested in satisfying the desire. Thus, we are willfully ignorant.

Yet if we pay attention to the effects of our actions, we can understand that each of these ten actions can be inverted, and converted into a powerful source of benefit for everyone. This is true of every harmful act and every desire: the energy it harnesses can be converted into benefit, if we know how. This is the scientific basis for the highest levels of spiritual instruction. Yet to succeed in that effort, the desire has to be completely transformed.

Consider the power of the ten harmful actions when they are converted through generosity and intelligence into virtuous action:

1. Life-giving: Instead of killing (life-taking), we act to protect the lives

of others in every way, especially spiritually and psychologically.

2. Generosity: Instead of stealing from others, we give to others, preferring to provide for others rather than ourselves. Parents can do this for children; why not extend this to everyone? What if our leaders in business, politics, and religion were to adopt this attitude? How different the world would be!

3. Sexual Purity: Instead of desire-based sexuality, we engage in spiritually-based sexuality, thus transforming our sexuality from something animal into something pure and Divine.

4. Truthfulness: Instead of lying to ourselves and others, we speak, think, and feel the truth, always, without exception.

5. Unifying Speech: Instead of acting to divide others, we foster unity and understanding, to strengthen relationships instead of weakening them.

6. Affirming Speech: Instead of thinking and speaking offensively, we express only what is positive, uplifting, and enlightening to others.

7. Wisdom Speech: Instead of senseless thought and speech, we say only what is true, useful, and important.

8. Happiness for Others: Instead of coveting what others have, we are grateful for what the Divine has given us, and we are grateful for what the Divine has given to others.

9. Cherishing: Instead of malice towards others, we cherish them and their well-being.

10. Right Views: Instead of protecting our ignorance, we embrace a cognizant awareness of reality, combined with an intelligent compassion for others, thereby cutting through appearances in order to see the facts.

Each harmful action weakens the consciousness. Each virtuous action strengthens the consciousness. The full development of the human being is accomplished when the consciousness reaches full strength and is capable of acting virtuously, for the benefit of everyone, at all times. This can only be reached by removing the causes of harmful action. Those causes can only be removed when they are seen and understood.

There are enumerable psychological aggregates within us, which are encoded energies that impel towards harmful action. If we want to overcome suffering, it is our duty to discover them, to analyze them, and to stop acting on them, instead adopting beneficial behaviors, thereby transforming sources of harm into sources of benefit. This cannot be accomplished automatically, or by merely intending to do good. Success in this effort depends on cognizance: conscious knowledge of reality, based on personal experience.

The Chain of Causality

The cycle of suffering is explained clearly in the Buddhist tradition by a formula which is called Pratityasamutpada.

pratitya: meeting, relying, depending

samutpada: arising

Pratityasamutpada is otherwise known as the Twelve Nidanas, the Twelvefold Chain of Causality, or Dependent Origination. There are many translations for the original terms, and all of them are correct. This is a very deep, very profound teaching, and it is not something your intellectual mind will ever fully grasp. Even when the Buddha's primary disciple Ananda claimed to understand it, the Buddha corrected him, saying:

> "Profound Ananda, this is Pratityasamutpada and profound does it appear. It is through not understanding, not penetrating this law, that this world resembles a tangled ball of thread... and that a man does not escape... suffering from the round of rebirth."

On another occasion he said:

> "Who so understands the
> Pratityasamutpada understands
> the Dharma [the path to lib-
> eration], and who so understands
> the Dharma understands the
> Pratityasamutpada."

Many people disregard this formula,
fearing it is too complicated or too intellectual. Truthfully, any teaching can
become too intellectual if we make it that.
It is necessary for us to understand the
teachings in a very profound way; these
structures and laws were not explained in
order for us to fill our minds with intellectual complications: they were given
for us to use in a practical way so that we
may escape suffering. That is their sole
purpose. If we take the teachings in an
intellectual way, that is our problem; it
does not mean the teachings themselves
are intellectual.

It is necessary for us to learn how to
understand the teachings consciously,
in all three brains: in the intellect, in the
heart, and in our actions. Typically, we
learn through the intellect first. That is
why you are reading this book.

When you understand it, when you grasp how it relates to your life, you enter into comprehension in the heart.

When you change your behaviors and act in a different manner, then you are beginning to grasp it in your motor-instinctive-sexual brain.

But your comprehension moves into levels beyond this when you have these three in equilibrium, and your every moment is filled with the awareness and respect for the laws expressed in these teachings: it becomes intuitive, spontane-

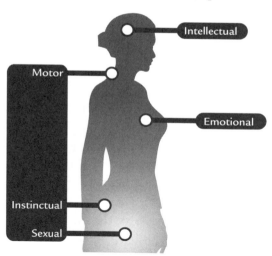

THE THREE BRAINS / FIVE CENTERS

ous, without thought or concept. At that point, you are living the teaching. It is then that you truly become conscious of the teachings.

So we should treat this knowledge with a lot of respect and without any preconceptions, and with the understanding that this teaching will need to be revisited again and again in order for there to be any real conscious understanding of it.

Remember always that we are beginners in this knowledge, and as children, as beginners, it takes patience and practice to learn. Reading something once does not mean we know it. As children in early schooling, we had to work slowly and consistently in order to learn what then may have seemed overwhelming to us: how to read, how to add, how to speak. The same is true of this knowledge for us now: we are children.

Returning to our theme, the whole formula of the twelve-fold chain of causality could be boiled down to a simple statement:

This being present, that arises;

Without this, that does not occur.

One example that you may have heard is that if fuel, air and ignition are all brought together, fire occurs. But if any of these elements are missing, there will be no fire. This is pretty simple, but this formula takes us into matters that are far from simple, and may even seem to some of us as being downright unacceptable.

In basic terms, the chain of causality teaches us that everything that is existent is dependent on something else. Nothing exists independently. This can lead us straight back to how the universe was created and what about a creator god, etc, but will not go into those questions in this book. Our purpose here is to focus on our lives and see the chain of causality in our own activities.

This twelve-fold chain is illustrated in the Tibetan "Bhava Chakra," the Wheel of Becoming, otherwise known as the Wheel of Samsara or the Wheel of Life. Images like this one are used as teaching and meditation aids. They are not meant to be literal in any sense: they are meant to aid the practitioner in visualizing concepts so that the imagination and the conscious-

The Wheel of Becoming, also called the Wheel of Samsara

ness can be utilized, rather than the intellectual mind.

Traditionally, the wheel is represented as a vast panorama in the grip of Yama, the Lord of Death, who represents delusion, ignorance, and the impermanence of all things that supports the whole mechanism of samsara, or the round of life and death.

In the center are three animals, eating one another, sustaining themselves on one another. They are the hub of the wheel, the central axis:

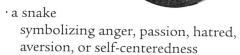

- a bird symbolizing craving and greed; desire

- a snake symbolizing anger, passion, hatred, aversion, or self-centeredness

- a pig or dog symbolizing ignorance and delusion

These three animals represent the process we have discussed until now: our unconscious state (ignorance, delusion) is sustained by desire (craving, greed, gluttony, lust) and aversion (hate, fear, etc). When we feed a craving we make it stronger; when we act on our aversions we strengthen them. This combination causes deeper lack of self-knowledge and the repetition of the entire cycle.

This process is the center of all suffering, and thus it is the center of the Wheel of Samsara. It is because of this process of selfish, unconscious desire that our life is what it is.

Everyone, manipulated by the subconscious elements in the mind, acts selfishly over and over again, under the influence of the urges of anger, greed, vanity, envy, laziness, pride, fear... Because of this, tremendous energies are put into motion, creating what we now experience as life, and we see as our modern world.

Unconscious thinking and feeling lead to unconscious action. The results are what you see in life: suicide, discontentment, brutality, rampant illness and physical suffering, disease, disability, accidents, disasters, rape, adultery, divorce, poverty, homelessness, anxiety, loneliness... Everything has been created by particular actions. Everything.

How does this manifest? The outer
ring of the wheel has twelve pictures,
twelve interlocking parts that illustrate
how energy moves: it is by this interlocking chain that the wheel has structure,
and it is upon this that the wheel moves.

1. Ignorance

We lack cognizant knowledge of cause
and effect. Indeed, because none of us
fully comprehend karma and the effects
we generate from moment to moment, we
are ignorant (represented
in the painting by a blind
man); we ignore the truth
of our actions, and we act
selfishly. We believe that
our sense of self is true,
that the mind is real, that
the mind is our true identity. That is
ignorance, because it is directly opposed
to the truth, and from that place we
unknowingly act out of balance, and create results.

2. Fashioning

Because of the condition of ignorance (1), our perceptions are inaccurate, thus transforming the energy of our perceptions into formations in our mind: memories, impulses, desires, fears, etc. The vast majority of these formations are below our ability to perceive them directly. Every tradition has names for these forma- tions in our mind: egos, aggregates, samskaras, sins, etc. This step is called Fashioning and is represented by a potter. These are forma- tions or crystallizations of energy, and they produce effects.

Because we have built a mass of formations in the mind, the energy of those formations is pure potentiality; that energy must produce effects: thus the condition is set for the next link.

3. Consciousness

The stored impressions in the mind are trapped energies that emerge when the conditions are right. These energies present a constant pressure towards expression, relative to their stored energy. The stored energy is trapped consciousness. Every enlightened being reached that state by freeing their consciousness from these submerged forms.

Effects we have put into motion must be completed. Energies must complete their cycle of manifestation, reaching balance. That is, our mind is in disharmony with nature.

Furthermore, the energy that we have locked in our mind—in the form of desires, fears, impulses, memories, cravings, etc.—causes the mind to remain in existence. Thus, when we die physically, these formations continue to exist in their level of nature (not physically), and create pressure to manifest themselves again. Thus, driven by those trapped energies, we are born in accordance to the nature of their energy. Our past actions determine our rebirth.

Consciousness (Sanskrit: vijnana) in this case is the necessity for existence. In our case, we had to be born because the energetic results of our past actions have not yet been fulfilled.

Thus, the energy trapped in our mental formations demands conditions for them to express themselves.

4. Name and Form

Both our free consciousness and the trapped consciousness work through our name (personality) and form (body).

From moment to moment, a confusing array of impulses is struggling to gain control of our "name and form" in order for them to manifest. Only very rarely do we consciously utilize name and form, unless we have been trained to self-observe.

This stage is usually represented in paintings by two men in a boat.

5. The Six Faculties

Consciousness (3) is the root of our perception, and perceives through the senses (5), which are in our "name and form" (4). The physical body has the senses of sight, hearing, smelling, tasting,

touching, and the sixth is the brain (and
personality) that coordinates them all.
These are represented in the painting as
six empty houses.

6. Sensual Contact

The physical senses transmit the
energy of the contact between the internal
and external worlds. This is the boundary
between senses and sense objects. Life
is received by the senses as impressions
before being received by the consciousness
(whether trapped or free).

7. Feeling

Sensations are received and are interpreted as pleasant, unpleasant, neutral.
This is where past effects begin to manifest in our lives, and are interpreted and
reacted to. The reception of sensations,
and the evaluation that occurs set up the
next link:

8. Craving or Thirst

As we label incoming sensations, we
experience delight, desire, and we crave

for pleasant experiences to be repeated over and over. This craving reactivates all our past cravings and passions. More and more passion is stimulated, more and more craving, which calls up more and more latent tendencies: thus by craving, we generate more craving, and by craving one thing we also crave other things, and desire grows and grows. This is the condition for the next link:

9. Grasping and Clinging

We, in our delusion, constantly chase pleasure, not realizing that everything is impermanent. We ignore the impermanence of all things, and chase after pleasure. We suffer because we are not content. Believing sensation will give us contentment, we chase sensations, but because sensations are impermanent, any contentment we find is short-lived, leaving us again in suffering. The pendulum always corrects its balance: the more we push toward pleasure, the more the pendulum pushes towards pain... As we grasp more and more after pleasure, we set the stage for...

10. Becoming

From the impulse of desire and in a state of ignorance, we seek more and more pleasure, acting out of balance with the reality of impermanence, and thus face more and more sensations we do not like, and want to avoid, and we seek more and more pleasure, all of which creates more and more thrust in the overall motion of the wheel...

In this stage, there is a massive energy propelling the arising of conditions that promote the arising of more and more latent formations, which in turn brings on the creation of further effects. All of this energy, this motion, must find fulfillment, because energy cannot be destroyed: it must manifest. This stage is usually depicted in the paintings as a pregnant woman who must give birth...

11. Birth

Because of the pressure created by past actions and their indelible effects, the whole sum of formations in the mind must re-appear... Thus, there is a constant manifestation of effects that must occur, and there is a tremendous impulse toward existence, toward manifestation... So, birth must continue...

However...

12. Decline and Death

All things are impermanent: they arise, and they pass away. It is this way with plants, animals,  lakes, continents, worlds, and it is this way with us, and with our actions. Every action brings its effect, and then passes away. Everything has its cycle.

During our life, we are propelled by the effects of our previous existences, and we add the actions of our new existence. Some debts are paid, others accrued. We enjoy the fruit of previous beneficial actions, or not. But inevitably, life ends, and without the balance of the scales being achieved. Death arrives, and since we did not clear up all of our energetic debts, we continue to carry the weight of our past actions, and thus must be reborn again in order to satisfy those debts...

"Verily I say unto thee, Thou shalt by no means come out thence, till thou hast paid the uttermost farthing." - Jesus of Nazareth, from Matthew 5

Thus, the whole cycle repeats. After death we are reborn, returned to the process of the wheel of cause and effect, propelled by past actions, by energies placed in the mind by unconscious, selfish, hateful, desirous action.

"Series do not exist for the Self-realized and diamantine Spirit; only the eternal present exists for him; he lives from instant to instant; he has freed himself from the Twelve Nidanas [pratityasamutpada]." - Samael Aun Weor

The center of the Wheel of Becoming

The Rotating Wheel

"A man's latent tendencies have been created by his past thoughts and actions. These tendencies will bear fruits, both in this life and in lives to come.

"So long as the cause exists, it will bear fruits—such as rebirth, a long or short life, and the experiences of pleasure and of pain." - Patanjali, Yoga Sutras

The twelve-fold chain of causality is the structure of the law of recurrence. All psychological formations are generators of recurrence: repeated events, situations, desires, fears, etc. For us, life is just a series of interlocking, repeating patterns, that we continually react to with ignorance, craving, and aversion, thereby deepening the repetition and ignorance.

Because we are psychologically asleep, we upset the balance of life, and we do not process the energies of life—perceptions, impressions—properly. These energies enter into us and are improperly digested, creating serious mental indigestion. These energies become latent, trapped, but must release their energy in some way: they must produce results, and they will do so in accordance to how they were made.

Anger can never bring contentment.

Lust can never bring satisfaction.

Envy can never give us equanimity.

Fear can never bring us peace.

So long as any such element remains in our mind, the consciousness within it is enslaved by its karmic cage, and is a victim to the churning suffering of the Wheel of Samsara.

> "Let no one say when he is tempted, 'I am tempted by God': for God cannot be tempted by evil and he himself tempts no one; but each person is tempted when he is lured and enticed by his own desire. Then desire when it has conceived gives birth to sin; and sin when it is full grown brings forth death." - James 1.13-15

To be free of the wheel is only possible when we are free of what belongs to it: all mechanical psychological elements.

So long as we have desire, we belong to the wheel of suffering and mechanicity.

So long as we have craving or aversion or fear or pride or gluttony or self-pity, we will suffer the repetition of the events that sustain them.

> "Truly, truly I say to you, everyone who commits sin is a slave to sin [because he is bound by the consequences of his actions, and will not be free until those debts are cleared]." - John 8.34

If anger is within us, suffering will occur in the form of the repetition of the events that sustains anger. If we react to those events with anger, we deepen the debt and the suffering to come.

If pride is within us, suffering will occur in relation to that pride.

If lust is within us, suffering will occur in relation to that lust.

Thus, anytime we suffer, we can determine the cause of that suffering by analyzing what in us is in pain.

In synthesis, the twelve-fold chain of causality outlines the essential structure of all action and consequence in the world of ignorance. When one comprehends that there is a fixed and determined structure to all ignorant action, one can then begin to use conscious action, upright action, and break the chain of causality.

All beings who have psychological formations (pride, lust, envy, fear, etc) are victims of the Wheel of Samsara.

Even most of the superior beings—whether we call them Angels, Buddhas, Gods—are subject to this wheel, because they remain dwelling in the manifested worlds, and have not reached absolute perfection: entry into the Abstract Space, called Ain in Hebrew, or Sunyata in Sanskrit. Very few have reached that level. That is why the Buddha warned Ananda.

As related in all our ancient mythologies, even the Gods have desire for power or pleasure, thus they too are enslaved by the wheel of cause and effect. The Buddhas of Nirvana, addicted to power and pleasure, have attachment, which will inevitably bring suffering.

Complete freedom from the Wheel of Samsara requires a completely free consciousness, totally awakened and without stain. Every aspirant to the Light must comprehend that in the Light there is nothing of the false self: there is no "I" as we can conceive of it: there is no pride, no desire, no worry, no attachment... To enter into that Perfection we must become like it. We must eliminate within ourselves that which cannot enter there. To do this, it is necessary that we comprehend very well the entire mechanism of suffering, and put in motion three factors that revolutionize our place in the universe.

THE WHEEL OF DESTINY

All Actions Come from Three Factors

Ignorance—psychological sleep—allows craving and aversion to modify our perception, thus giving rise to suffering. We can only change our suffering by changing this fundamental root. Unfortunately, we try to change our suffering by changing our circumstances, not their origin. Whatever is happening around us was caused by what is within us. If we seriously want to change our circumstances, we have to change our psychology first.

> "There can be a modification of circumstances and of problems, but they will never cease repeating themselves and they will never have a final solution.

> "Life is a wheel that turns mechanically with all the pleasant and unpleasant experiences, always recurring.

> "We cannot stop the wheel, the good or bad circumstances always process

themselves mechanically. We can only change our attitude toward the events of life." - Samael Aun Weor

Everything changes, all the time. We make choices all the time, choices that can create change. So it is possible for anyone to change, and to come into balance.

For energy to move, there must be three factors engaged. This is a universal law as fundamental as cause and effect. Every cause is made possible by three factors. Every effect emerges because three factors were engaged.

The three factors are relative to the level in which they are acting. At the most subtle level of existence, they are the trinity symbolized in every religion. In us, here and now, the three factors are visible in many places: our three nervous systems, our three brains (intellect, heart, and body), in how we create children (man, woman, and sex), etc.

At the heart of the wheel of samsara are three factors: craving, aversion, and ignorance. These three factors create our suffering. To conquer suffering, those three factors must be transformed consciously into three factors that liberate us from the wheel:

1. Death: the elimination of the psychological generators of harmful action; i.e.: free the trapped consciousness

2. Birth: the empowerment of beneficial action; i.e.. awaken and develop the free consciousness

3. Sacrifice: action to help others become free of suffering; i.e.. put the consciousness to work for the benefit of humanity

These three factors are engaged through awakening and developing the consciousness. When the free consciousness is awake, here and now, these three factors can be put in motion, originating an entirely new way of life.

David gegen Goliath, by Gebhard Fugel (1863–1939)

Willpower

No matter how desperate our situation in life, we still retain some amount of free will. Even if we are crippled, imprisoned, starved, ignored, and forgotten, we still retain the ability to choose how to react to life; that is, even if all of our other faculties are otherwise restricted, our consciousness can make choices. Any choice is an action with consequences. Free will is made possible by karma, and likewise, karma is made possible by free will. In other words, consciousness and cause and effect are intimately related. You cannot have one without the other.

Even when our consciousness is restricted and bound by the consequences of its previous actions, there always remains the possibility to change directions. One simply needs the will to do it.

Willpower is consciousness in action.

Unfortunately, since our consciousness is trapped in a multiplicity of desires, we are filled with a multiplicity of conflicting wills. This is a cause of suffering:

we contradict ourselves constantly, and often are completely unaware of it.

Nonetheless, when a desire is strong enough, enormous willpower is directed to fulfill that desire. An addict demonstrates incredible willpower to feed his addiction. He can overcome incredible obstacles, and withstand enormous suffering, just to feed his desire.

To reach the heights of spiritual development requires every atom of willpower we can muster. This is the basis for the true spiritual war: it is between our free consciousness and the desires that have trapped the majority of our consciousness. Now you can understand the meaning of the story of David and Goliath.

The youth David is able to conquer the giant warrior Goliath because of two factors: his faith in God, and his use of a stone.

Even though karma is a law of nature that balances energy, it is not mechanical. The law of karma is a conscious law: it is managed and directed by conscious intelligence, what some call God, and others call Gods. The law of karma is not a blind, mechanical law.

"Intelligence governs the whole Cosmos, whether it is within the infinitely small or within the infinitely large. Intelligence exists in the Macrocosm and in the Microcosm, in a system of worlds, in a beehive or in an anthill. Cosmic Intelligence abides precisely in each particle of this great creation." - Samael Aun Weor, Gnostic Anthropology

Everything in nature has a spiritual aspect, and all of that is managed by an intelligence that is far beyond our theories or beliefs. Every atom in existence has consciousness. So does a galaxy, a sun, a solar system... even the universe. Truly, on the stage of existence, we are incredibly insignificant. Nonetheless, since we have consciousness, we are connected to the whole, and have a purpose to fulfill.

Cause and effect is the teacher that guides us towards our purpose. By learning how to act properly, we acquire knowledge, understanding, and power to act more effectively. Through action, we too can become an angel, a buddha, a Master. Such a being is a Master of

Conscious Action: conscious willpower in motion.

The Source of Action

Every being has a spiritual root that is far beyond our psychology, our soul, spirit, or mind. Our root is a spiritual star, a radiating light that is beyond any type of individuality or sense of I. Some religions call this root intelligence God, Allah, Adi Buddha, Ain Soph, Tao, Brahma, and many other names. All point towards the same fundamental reality, about which all of us are in the utmost state of ignorance. Yet, our deepest inner reality is One Law: the will of That Which Is.

When we do not know the will of our Innermost Being, then our actions are mistaken, and we acquire the consequences of our actions. Only those who awaken consciousness and free themselves from self-will (desire) can know and act upon the will of That Which Is. Then, they are in harmony with the infinite, and have all the powers of the Divine at their disposal, to act for the benefit of suffering beings.

The will of the Divine is the First Law. It is the One Law. To know and act upon this law is to know and converse with God. Moses, Mohammed, Krishna, Padmasambhava, Tsong Khapa, Buddha, and many other masters performed the will of the One Law.

It is the ultimate goal of each living creature to attain re-union (religare, yoga) with its primordial source. Yet, this does not happen automatically. It is a work of willpower. Nature does not make Gods, only animals, plants, and minerals. A fully developed human organism commands nature inside of him and outside of him. Such a person is not a slave of nature, but a King or Queen of Nature. His divinity is the presence of the One Law within.

For those who have not awakened consciousness enough to access the One Law, the Divine provides a guide to reach that level: it is called the Second Law, and is constituted by the instructions given in the heart of every genuine religion. To reach the First Law, we first must live by the Second Law. Those who reach the First Law are no longer bound by the Second Law. This is why many great masters have performed actions that contradict the Second Law.

A being becomes a true master by incarnating and perfecting the First Law, the Being, in themselves. Usually, those who follow the Second Law condemn the incarnations of the First Law, because they cannot understand them.

This First Law is the will of our own Innermost Being, not others: an action that is lawful for our own Being, and for us to perform, may be wrong for another person. This is how we can understand the seemingly wrong actions of masters like Joan of Arc, who led armies and killed, and performed many actions which, according to the Second Law, are "wrong." Yet she was acting under the direct commands of her own Inner Law: therefore what she was doing was right. This is why we should never judge the actions of another.

> "I would rather die than do something which I know to be a sin, or to be against God's will." - Joan of Arc

To conquer suffering, every being must act in accordance with the One Law within themselves. Yet how can we act in accordance with this Law if we do not even know who or what the Being is?

Every soul who lives, breathes, works, and acts in ignorance of their true purpose in life is wasting their time; not only that, they are deepening their own suffering, because their every action is performed in ignorance of their own inner Law.

We who live and act in ignorance of our inner spiritual and psychological root commit crimes daily because we act without knowing the right way to act. Not only do we contradict the First Law, we contradict the Second Law. For this to change we need to awaken consciousness from moment to moment, and listen to our conscience.

Our conscience—intuition—tells us right from wrong, and how to act, and when. This is the first step towards negotiating our karma.

The One Law within us guides us through the heart. Yet, to hear that guidance, we need a quiet mind.

Only you can know what is right for you to do, because only you are directly connected to your Divine Source. No one outside of you can ever give you advice more accurate than what you can acquire within.

The Innermost guides through the voice of the silence. To hear that voice, our mind must be silent.

To hear that voice, we must consciously remember to listen for it from moment to moment.

Then, when hearing that guidance, knowing intuitively, consciously, how and when to act, we can change the course of our life, under the guidance of our Innermost Being. This cannot happen if we are influenced by our desire.

"No servant can serve two masters..."
- Jesus, Luke 16

In many cases, we already know what we should do, but we do not want to do it, because we want to pursue the will of our desires.

Humanity is enslaved by desire. Humanity's actions are motivated by craving, aversion, and ignorance, the three factors that create suffering. Humanity suffers because the source of our action is desire, self-will. Humanity ignores the urges of conscience, preferring to listen to the urges of desire in the form of lust, pride, envy, jealousy, fear, etc.

To act on divine will, we must deny our own self-will.

> "If any man will come after me, let him first deny himself..." - Jesus of Nazareth

By denying our desires and doing what we know is right, we perform a superior action that overcomes inferior actions. This is the first step in the negotiation of our karma.

Karma is not a mechanical law. It is managed by conscious intelligence. The first manager of cause and effect in us is our Innermost Being. When we do what is right, we are rewarded by our Being. When we act improperly, we receive what we deserve, as given to us by our Innermost Being.

> "Behold, happy [is] the man whom God corrects..." - Job 5

Three Kinds of Action

There are three types of action:

1. Actions emerging from the law of accidents.

2. Actions driven by the law of Recurrence; actions always repeated in each existence.

3. Actions intentionally determined by the will of the unconditioned consciousness.

We assume our actions are conscious. We presume that because we are not in bed sleeping, then we are awake and able to make conscious choices. Unfortunately, however, this is not the case. The truth is that our consciousness is asleep. Even when our body is active, our consciousness is passive, dreaming, distracted; it is rarely present and awake. Thus, most of our "choices" are not really choices at all, but merely reactions to circumstances.

We have a small amount of "free will." We are able to make some small choices for ourselves. However, life for us is such that we do not have complete freedom: we are swept along by our karma. Everything important in life just happens to us.

If you objectively, disinterestedly, examine your life and the major circumstances, were they a matter of choice? Did you choose your parents? Many people like to think that we choose our parents, but really, who is conscious of having made such a choice? Did you choose your race, your sex, your level of intelligence, your heredity, your circumstances as a child? If we are suffering in this life, do you really believe we chose that suffering? Would we really choose to have our children suffer? Our loved ones? Why would anyone chose to have so much pain? If we choose our life circumstances, then why do we all not want what we have, and long to have what we do not?

The idea that people "choose" their modern lives is a ludicrous theory invented by new-age dreamers: there is absolutely nothing in any true teaching that indicates such a belief. They believe it because it makes them feel better about the terrifying reality of karma and suffering.

We do not want to face the facts: that human beings suffer intensely, and to our blind eyes, without good reason. We are blind to the truth because we are asleep psychologically, and cannot see the karma behind the suffering.

We are victims of our own harmful actions. Our circumstances are a result of our karma, or in other words, our past actions. Everything in our lives is as it is because of our previous actions, and because the conditions are ripe for the results to manifest.

Even when we make a "choice," most of the time, we really have no choice.

The events and circumstances of our life are nothing more than a series of repeating patterns that we set in motion unconsciously, and react to unconsciously.

For the vast majority of humanity, their actions are accidents and recurrence. Very few individuals know how to act with the will of the free consciousness.

Conditions

The circumstances of our life—which are the results of previous actions—have emerged because the conditions allow it.

As we have stated, for the result of any action to manifest, the conditions must be conducive. The results blossom when the conditions are ripe.

If we want to consciously manage the fruit of our life, we need to influence the conditions of our life.

If you want to grow a garden, you need the right conditions. It would be very difficult or impossible to grow fruit in an inhospitable climate. Similarly, if you want to have a successful business, you need to position it in the right conditions. Spiritual success also depends on conditions that support it.

Though we are burdened with karma and we must face the results of all of our previous actions, this is not something that unfolds purely mechanically. There still remains in all of us some small margin of free will: the ability to choose.

The first step to negotiating our karma is by choosing to behave in a better way. The best way to do that is to provide ourselves with conditions that support our decisions.

If you want to stop drinking alcohol, the first step is to stop going to bars, parties, and places where drinking is encouraged. If you remain in the conditions that support the action of drinking, then drinking is not only likely, but inevitable.

Spending time with drug-using friends places you amongst the conditions that encourage the desire to use drugs. If you do not want to take drugs, then you should not put yourself in those conditions.

If you place certain things together, then there will be specific results. To get the results you want, work with the proper conditions.

If you spend time with peaceful, serene people, those conditions will have an effect on you. If you spend time in bars, those conditions will have an effect on you. This is unavoidable.

If you want to become chaste, you must create conditions that support chastity.

Effects can only manifest under supportive conditions. Examine the conditions in your life, and be more conscious of where you take yourself, and what kind of influences you are choosing.

THE PARABLE OF THE BLIND LEADING THE BLIND,
BY PIETER BRUEGEL THE ELDER

Accidents

Those who have their consciousness asleep are subject to the law of accidents. Those who have their consciousness asleep are blind. The blind crash into each other, and accidents result.

A sleeping consciousness daydreams, thinks, imagines, fantasizes, and in general is rarely here and now.

Modern life is characterized by an extreme state of distraction. Drivers of cars are driving, eating, talking, and thinking of something else, all at the same time. This is why those drivers have accidents: they are not paying attention to what they are doing. They are asleep.

If you are not paying attention to the present moment, but are absorbed in thinking about something and you step out in front of a car, and the driver of the car is daydreaming, he will hit and kill you; that is caused by the law of accidents. You were both asleep, and suffering is the result.

A large percentage of our lives is moved about by the law of accidents. We are like a log drifting on a sea of cause and effect, tossed from here to there. Asleep, we have no ability to direct ourselves through life, and so everything just happens to us.

This is not the cruelty of God or the absence of God's presence: it is our rejection of his ability to help us, because without the presence of the consciousness, God cannot be present in us. Therefore, we need to learn how to be conscious, to remember Him, so he can help us escape the painful surging of the sea of life.

By being present, here and now, continually, we become attentive to what is happening, and can act accordingly. This is how we reduce the occurrence of accidents in our life.

Recurrence

When we react mechanically to the process of cause and effect, we feed the cycle, and it repeats.

When a situation occurs that brings out our anger, and we become angry, and act from anger, we feed the anger and invest more energy into the situation, which gives it longevity and the potential to repeat.

When we feed lust, it grows stronger, and wants to repeat the sensations it enjoys.

When we feed our envy, it grows stronger, and repeatedly demands to be fed.

Our mind is filled with an incredible number of subjective psychological formations. Each formation is a mechanical structure: a machine with limited functionality, that can only repeat itself.

For example, remember a situation where you felt that you looked bad to others; perhaps you were embarrassed by your clothes, your accent, your lack of education, or something like that. You reacted, feeling shame, and attempted to cover your shame by doing something to boost your pride. Perhaps you attacked the one who embarrassed you. Afterward, you told yourself that you were justified. This scenario was unconscious action that will rise again when the conditions allow. It will repeat. The trapped energy will emerge, and if we respond as usual, we will strengthen it.

Death does not end the repetition of desires, events, scenes... The energy of cause and effect must be settled, so we are reborn, to repeat once more the cycles of our desires. As circumstances allow, the cycles will repeat. If at age 25 we submitted to our lust, in our next life, the same event will repeat. If we repeat it unconsciously again, we make it stronger.

This is the law of recurrence.

Impregnated within all those formations are the conditions of their creation, conditions that will repeat themselves mechanically, over and over and over. What happened in one life will happen in the next, in exactly the same way and at exactly the same time, in the next life, and it will continue from life to life, as long as we continue reacting in the same way.

Observe yourself, and you will see that in situation after situation you react in the same way, all the time, because of inner pressures, inner pain, inner urges, anger, fear, envy... and there is maybe a feeling that you can escape the situation, or that you are justified in acting this way... The sad truth is that repetition of circumstance will continue as long as we repeat our reactions. We spin the wheel ourselves.

If you react with anger every time you are confronted with anger, then you are spinning the wheel onward. You are feeding it, and condemning yourself to repetition. And because we are all doing this, because we are all reacting to inner cravings and inner aversions, and we are doing this back and forth, you and me, repeating situations together, we are karmically tied and will continue meeting and repeating situations, deepening our troubles.

If Greg and I find ourselves in a situation where his pride needs to be superior to me, and he reacts to that, and makes sure that he looks better than me, and I am hurt by it, my pride is hurt, and my anger is engaged, and both of us are reacting to the quiet urgings of the mind, then we are creating formations in our individual minds, and we are creating a karmic link: the formations in my mind are linked to him, and his to me. And so, not only will his pride become stronger and seek to feed itself again, but it will do so in the same way, at the same time, with me, in the next life. Naturally, this is complicated, and if I am not reborn or some other circumstance overrides it, then it will change. But this is the tendency. Thus you can see, that karmic links are deep and subtle, and we are all in the midst of a vast and complex web of interrelations, all of which depends upon unconsciousness, or mechanical reactions to the mind and to external circumstances.

The repeating events manifest in a myriad of ways: but if there is karma to be paid, the event will be inverted: if we killed, then we will be killed.

"All those events of repeated existences are always accompanied by good and bad consequences, in accordance with the law of cause and effect.

"The murderer will return to see himself in the horrifying occasion of murdering, but he will be murdered; the thief will once again see himself with the same opportunity of stealing, but will be thrown in jail; the bandit will feel the same desire of running, of using his legs for crime, but he will not have legs, he will be born invalid or will lose them in some tragedy. The blind person will want from birth to see the things of life, those that possibly led him to cruelty, but he will not be able to see. The woman will love the same husband of her previous life, he whom she possibly abandoned on the sick bed to go off with any other person, but now the drama will be repeated inversely and the object of her love will leave with another woman, abandoning her..." - Samael Aun Weor, Yes, There is a Hell, a Devil, and Karma...

Many people, seduced by their own need for love, rush into relationships, feeling that "this is the one!" "I feel like I have known him forever!" "We were made for each other." We believe we have found our soul mate, when in truth, in most cases, we have found a karmic relationship, one that intoxicates us with a sense of belonging and familiarity, but which will later prove to be a vehicle of karma that we must pay.

This does not mean that we should avoid relationships: it means that we need to become conscious of them. We need a spouse, yet we need to be with the spouse that our Being chooses for us.

If I am trying to awaken, and I am not reacting to the urgings of my mind, then I can choose what to do. If I am married, and a woman shows up who entices me, and seems like a better partner to me, my "soul mate," I may have enough consciousness awakened to see that she there because of recurrence: a repeated cycle of karmic tendencies. I may see that she has come to me again and again, from life to life, and each time, I chose to go with her, and each time I did that I fed the cause of the situation, and deepened the karmic link. This knowledge helps me to avoid deepening the suffering of everyone involved.

"The life of each of one of us is a living film, which at death we carry with us to eternity.

"Each of us carries his film with him, and returns with it, to project it once again on the screen of a new existence.

"The repetition of dramas, comedies, and tragedies is a fundamental axiom of the law of Recurrence.

"In each new existence, the same circumstances are always repeated. The actors in these recurring scenes are those people who live within us, the "I's."

"If we disintegrate those actors, those "I's" which originate the ever-repeated scenes of our life, then the repetition of such circumstances becomes more than impossible.

"Obviously, without actors there cannot be scenes; this is irrefutable, undeniable. Thus, we can liberate ourselves from the laws of Return and Recurrence; thus we can truly free ourselves." - Samael Aun Weor, Revolutionary Psychology

The way out of this is conscious action, right action. If you can observe yourself, and really become aware of the motivations in your heart, the fear in your thinking, the hatred in your mind, then you can stop reacting, and you can choose to act consciously. You can take responsibility for the situation, and act properly.

The Wheel of Life is a map of all of this. Upon the Wheel we see not only the root of all of life and death, the Three Poisons of hatred, ignorance and desire, but we see the chain of causality, and we see an inner ring of humans rising and falling, passing from life to death and back again... becoming more conscious or less conscious, and thus passing between levels of existence. All the while, we are trapped in a web of karmic bonds, pushed by elements that want to express themselves through our minds, hearts and actions, elements that want to repeat their inner nature through recurrence. Even when we die, those elements remain with us, and their combined weight pushes us into another life.

Return

"This vast universe is a wheel. Upon it are all creatures that are subject to birth, death, and rebirth. Round and round it turns, and never stops. It is the wheel of Brahman. As long as the individual self thinks it is separate from Brahman, it revolves upon the wheel in bondage to the laws of birth, death, and rebirth. But when through the grace of Brahma it realizes its identity with him, it revolves upon the wheel no longer. It achieves immortality." - Svetasvatara Upanishad (Prabhavananda), 118

If from life to life we continually protect and nourish our desires, fears, and resentments, and deal with life through anger, jealousy, vanity, and pride, then we build tremendous formations in our minds that exert control over us continually. Then we die... and are reborn, propelled by the contents of our psyche, in accordance to the weight in our minds.

Thus, we return to a new body, whose every feature and circumstance is determined by our previous actions. Our parents, our social status, country, language, religion, education—everything—is a result of the cause and effect we established in our previous existences. Everything we are now is a result of what we did before.

We return in order to experience the effects of our previous actions—to exhaust our karma. Unfortunately, we tend to add to our karma more than pay it, thus from existence to existence we tend to deepen our debts and mistakes, rather than reducing them.

Just like a drop of water rolling to the edge of a leaf, at a certain moment the water hangs on the edge, then falls. So it us with us.

Return can only happen if our karmic debts are not too deep. Once they reach a certain critical mass, the droplet falls: we receive no more physical bodies. Nature takes our mind in order to purify it. Most religions call this process hell.

Hell: Nature's Recycling

Nature will balance the imbalance we created, by purifying our minds for us. Nature purifies us in the same manner that it breaks down everything: through decay, degeneration, destruction. This is the Second Death, mentioned in the Bible and in the Egyptian mysteries. This is Hell.

Hell is nature's recycling plant, where the consciousness is freed from the formations we have built around it. But nature, as you can observe in the processes of life all around us, works slowly. To be purified by nature is a very slow, painful process. As painful as our karma may be in the physical world, it is very easy and shallow compared to the suffering endured in hell.

Therefore, it is truly in our best interest to pay our debts now, to clear our mind of all impurity, so that nature will have nothing to cleanse from us. The choice is ours. It is painful to see the ugliness in our minds, the hatred in our hearts, but it is less painful than nature's method of purification.

Already, we see that humanity is entering hell, even while still in physical bodies. The degeneration of this humanity has reached a stage never before seen on this planet. The widespread corruption and criminality—so celebrated and recommended by governments, media, and artists—is accelerating the decay of our civilization. In response, nature is beginning to cleanse this planet, by intensifying the conditions around us through extreme weather, natural disasters, diseases, illnesses, and a multiplicity of sufferings heretofore unknown.

The only way to avoid being caught in the maelstrom is to negotiate your karma. You can do this starting right now, by realizing the types of karma that are affecting you, and acting appropriately.

Individual Karma

We as individuals owe for the harmful actions we have performed in the past. We suffer in many different ways in accordance with our own wrong actions.

Most of the suffering in our life is due to harmful actions we performed in the past. By learning to stop our bad habits and automatic reactions, we can reduce and eventually end altogether the continuation of these sufferings.

Marriages, jobs, family situations, problems with money, health, children, etc. are generally due to our individual karma.

"The worst genres of sicknesses are those which are engendered by karma. Variola is the result of hatred, diphtheria is the fruit of fornication from past lives. Cancer is also the result of fornication.

"Tuberculosis or white pestilence is the result of atheism and materialism from past lives. Cruelty engenders blindness at birth. Rachitis is the child of materialism. Malaria comes from egotism, etc. Hundreds of other sicknesses have their origin in the evil actions from our past lives." - Samael Aun Weor, Occult Medicine and Practical Magic

Individuals who are enjoying their last opportunity in a physical body, and previously did a lot of good deeds but did not awaken consciousness, are paid what they are owed in full. Such persons are often wealthy, loved, and surrounded by everything one could want in life, but have little or no spiritual values. When the compensation for their good deeds has been fully paid, they die, and nature recycles them.

Family Karma

Every family, as a group of intense interaction, creates a complex and deeply interwoven web of action and consequence. Many families have been together for hundreds of years, deepening and intensifying their suffering from life to life, and occasionally sacrificing for each other in beautiful ways.

Families share a common psychological link. Every family is designed by the cause and effect stream of each family member, who collectively have a strong psychological affinity. Although many families embrace their idiosyncrasy as "unique" or "special," it is actually just karma, cause and effect. Thus we see families who are proud, arrogant, ashamed, or insensitive, lustful, addictive, intellectual, artistic, mechanically-oriented, etc.

In family karma, the roles often switch: it is common to return as one's own grandchild. Usually, this is due to strong recurrence in the family. The cruel father is born as the child of his own child, in order to have done to him what he had done to others. If the new parent expresses his own resentment through brutality and cruelty, the cycle will invert and repeat again. Thus we can understand those families that are torn by murder, rape, and other horrible crimes.

Group Karma

Groups act, and receive the effects of their actions. Every club, church, business, movement, political party, school, city, region, state, country, etc. is a producer and receiver of cause and effect. We see these groups receive the consequences of their actions, as some groups receive benefits, and others suffer. Groups pay in the form of earthquakes, epidemics, political enslavement, poverty, wars, etc. Observe how a natural disaster or war can obliterate one group while leaving another untouched. Diseases sweep through communities, leaving some unaffected, and others devastated.

In all of our previous lives, we have been countrymen, members of churches, armies, schools, militias, etc. The actions of those groups generated consequences that affect us, relative to our degree of participation.

Those who pay taxes bear responsibility for how the taxes are used. Naturally, the politicians and government employees who spend the tax money to pay for war and killing bear more responsibility, while those who do the killing acquire even more. This is a complex mixture of individual and group karma.

Individuals who owe group karma are freed from the debt only when the originator of the action has been destroyed. That is, the element in the psyche that caused the original action must be removed. The only way to accomplish this is through very deep comprehension and meditation.

Karma Saya

Karma saya is in relation with our use of sex and the atomic seed.

"If a woman leaves her husband, then she is not free from him, neither is he free from her, since when a marital union is already established, this remains for the whole of eternity." - Paracelsus, Homunculis

"Really, the human personality is contained within the semen, because the semen is the astral liquid of the human being. For this reason, every sexual union is indissoluble.

"The man who has sexual contact with a married woman remains in a permanent bond with part of the karma of her husband, for that motive. Fluidly, the two husbands of the woman are connected by means of sex." - Samael Aun Weor, Occult Medicine and Practical Magic

Karma saya is a very potent form of cause and effect, since it is originated from the most potent energy we utilize: sexual energy. Each use of sexual energy has an unimaginable impact, and truly cannot be matched by any other expenditure of energy. What other action can create life? Sexual energy is the basis of life. Thus, the consequences for its use are far more extensive than any other action. This is why every religion in the world emphasized the importance of controlling our sexual energy.

The most painful forms of suffering are the consequences for abusing sexual energy. In most cases, these are sufferings of the heart, due to betrayal, adultery, rape, etc.

Karma Duro

Karma duro is related to fornication: the waste of sexual energy. This is the only form of karma that is not negotiable.

"All manner of sin may be forgiven except the sin against the Holy Spirit."

Sexual degeneration, fornication, cannot be forgiven because the karma must play itself out through pain. Fornication, the indulgence in self-willed pleasure, is paid only through pain.

Cancer is caused by fornication.

Katancia

Those who awaken consciousness acquire powers and abilities that naturally create more powerful effects. Thus, angels, gods, and masters bear more responsibility for their actions. For them, the law is called Katancia.

Those who developed to some degree but then fell fall under the judgment of this law. Fallen angels, fallen bodhisattvas, acquire huge debts for betraying their duty and humanity.

Katancia is the superior karma that judges the children of the Gods. This is the law that applies to the Buddhas and Bodhisattvas.

The End of Karma

All creatures exist in order to come to know their own Innermost Being, their Inner Star.

Those who cycle through existence from life to life without awakening and developing their consciousness are simply cycling through aeons of suffering. They accumulate karma and they pay karma, and in the end, they gain nothing because they never gain cognizant knowledge.

Those who want to develop all of their latent abilities and incarnate their inner divinity must settle their accounts with the law of karma, neither owing nor being owed.

There is a stage at which one must not owe any karma, nor be owed. One must have perfect equilibrium. Only then can one go on...

Those who want to know their Innermost Being must learn how to negotiate their karma.

For the beginners, each step of development is made by paying karma.

The initiates of the Spiral Path pay their karma slowly, over millennia.

The initiates of the Straight Path pay their karma now, rapidly, without hesitation. Such initiates are very, very rare. Very few choose the Straight Path, for fear of facing the entirety of their karma.

Most creatures are on neither path, and instead are just being processed in great cycles by nature, and in the end, return to their source having gained nothing but millennia of suffering.

There are also many on the devolving path, enslaved by nature but awakening consciousness, who seek to accumulate as much karma as possible, motivated by the mistaken notion that the condensed, descending energy of their evil deeds will eventually propel them to the heights of the Light. This is equivalent to saying that the more pain we inflict on ourselves and others, the more pleasure we will receive. This is insanity. There are many on this planet who eagerly pursue that path. They suffer a deep ignorance regarding cause and effect. They attempt to trick a law that cannot be tricked.

Forgiveness and Redemption

Karma is medicine that is applied to us for our own good. If there were no karma, everything would be much worse than it is now. But because there are consequences for our actions, we are kept in check, and we are forced to learn. We learn by suffering the consequences of harmful action, and being rewarded for our beneficial actions.

Nonetheless, karma can also be forgiven. Just as we can forgive others for their debts, so too can the divine forgive us ours. Forgiveness is a jewel in the crown of consciousness.

Karma is not a blind, merciless law. If it were, God would not be merciful. But God is merciful. God is love, and, in fact, love is the law.

Karma can seem harsh, bitter, even cruel, but that is what we need in order to see the truth in ourselves. The medicine for the soul does not taste like sugar. Yet, it is still given from love.

When repentance is absolute, punishment is unnecessary. When we fully comprehend the suffering caused by harmful actions, renunciation of those actions is effortless. Then, we can dissolve the psychological source of those impulses to harmful action. If the source of harm no longer exists in us, punishment is not needed. The one who has no anger cannot become angry, thus there is no need to punish the person for their anger.

Forgiveness is given when we are no longer capable of committing the crime. To be forgiven, we must cleanse ourselves of the elements that want to perform harmful actions. Yet, if we still are interested in committing the crime, we do not deserve forgiveness.

Purification

To reach purification from any harmful psychological element, we need to work with three defined stages:

1. Observation

2. Judgment

3. Elimination

The harmful elements in us do not deserve forgiveness or mercy. They are the cause of suffering, and can only produce suffering. They must be eliminated.

During observation, we pay close attention to how the element attempts to influence our three brains: intellect (thoughts), heart (emotions), and body (impulses, desires). Observation is a process of collecting facts, not theories or guesses. At trial, only facts are considered.

Observation that only gathers data through the five senses of the physical body is akin to a detective who lacks evidence from the scene of the crime. The scene of the crime in us is psychological. Thus, we need to gather psychological evidence. That is, we need to observe the facts of our thoughts, feelings, and impulses as they actually happened. For this to be effective, we need to gather data in two ways:

1. By observing the element that is active in us in any given moment
2. By scientifically reviewing the scene of action; this is a technique of meditation

Without conscious observation of ourselves from moment to moment, we cannot gather the facts regarding how our psychological gang operates.

Without profound meditation on the actions of those elements, we cannot perceive their inner, psychological roots.

Observation and meditation must accompany one another in our daily life.

Observation must be active, awake, and continuous.

Meditation must be perfectly relaxed, totally withdrawn from the exterior world, and capable of profoundly clear visualization.

Both observation and meditation have a single goal: to gather information.

For observation and meditation to be effective, they must be free of the influence of any psychological element. In other words, our point of view must be the work of free, unconditioned consciousness that observes without pride, shame, envy, lust, craving, aversion, gluttony, greed, laziness, or any type of self-will.

After we have gathered sufficient facts for analysis, we can judge the element and condemn it.

Judgment occurs when we are convinced of the crime and its cause, and repentance emerges spontaneously.

When we unable to act on the impulses of the element, we have comprehended it. An element of anger is comprehended when, upon suddenly seeing the former object of our anger, we do not feel anger, but love. This shows that the element of anger that previously influenced us cannot any longer, and is ready to be eliminated.

Elimination is given by the divine. Elimination of psychological formations is performed by the Divine Mother in us. She is able to accomplish this if we have saved our sexual energy and dedicated it for her use.

She, the Divine Mother, has the power to create life and to take it. She is Athena, Kali, Tara, Mary, Hera, Aphrodite. She is Kundalini.

Those who do not eliminate the psychological errors by their own will are subjected to purification in hell. That is the domain of Persephone, Hekate, the Goddess of the Underworld, who oversees the purification of conditioned consciousness.

Therefore, whether by our will during our daily life now, or against our will while descending into hell after death, the Divine Mother cleanses us of our errors. It is better to do it on our own. This is a superior action that originates enormous benefits. One of those benefits is that She can forgive us of many kinds of karma. She is our mother, and loves us dearly. She does not want to see us suffer.

Judgment

Everything in nature has intelligence: rocks, plants, animals, etc. There is a living spirit behind it all. This is also true of karma. Karma is managed by conscious, active, intelligent forces, but these forces are far beyond the comprehension of our intellectual minds.

Karma is managed by conscious intelligence. All great religions and mystical traditions teach that we must account for our actions in the end: there will be a time when we must face a judge, a tribunal, and answer for each action of our lives.

The gods and goddesses of the ancient religions are not myths; many are awakened beings, buddhas, or angels, that are still active in different regions of consciousness. The vast force of karma is managed by a being whom the Egyptians called Anubis, the jackal-masked god. Anubis is a conscious, awakened being who has the duty of managing karma. He is assisted by 42 judges or lords of the law, who are also awakened beings. He wears a mask to hide his face, in order to be impartial.

The Egyptian mysteries teach about the measurement of the karma of the dead. The deceased person is brought before a great tribunal, and the weight of his karma, symbolized by his heart, is measured against a feather. Anubis attends the scale, the balance of actions and consequences, and the scale that measures our deeds. All of our actions are recorded in a book. And so we are judged: if we were self-serving and acted without care, then we owe and must pay. And if we served others, and did good deeds, then we are owed, and must be paid.

When we die, all of our actions will be examined. Let us not have any fantasies about this. Let us examine ourselves honestly, and look at even the little we know about this life, not even accounting for all of our past lives: how would we come out?

"We demand fidelity from the spouse when we ourselves have been adulterers in this life or in previous lives.

"We ask for love when we have been merciless and cruel.

"We demand comprehension when we have never known how to comprehend anyone, when we have never learned to see the other person's point of view.

"We long for immense good fortune when we have always been the origin of many misfortunes.

"We would have liked to have been born in a very beautiful home with many comforts, when in past lives we did not know how to provide a home and beauty for our children.

"We protest against persons who insult us when we have always insulted everyone who surrounds us.

"We want our children to obey us when we have never known how to obey our parents.

"Slander annoys us terribly when we were always slanderers and filled with world with pain.

"Gossip upsets us, we do not want anyone to gossip about us, however we were always involved in gossip and backbiting, talking badly about our fellowmen, mortifying the lives of others.

"That is, we always demand what we have not given; in all our former lives we were evil and we deserve the worst, but we suppose that we should be given the best." - Samael Aun Weor

We live life as if we had an unlimited balance credit card that we never have to pay back. It is necessary that we begin to see that this is not realistic, nor is it beneficial for anyone, including ourselves. Clearly, we all have made many mistakes. What can we do to negotiate our karma? When we are brought before the Great Judge, what will we have to offer, to pay for all the evil things we have done?

Negotiation

We should never protest against our karma. When life brings us problems, challenges, suffering, do not complain. Instead, learn how to transform it. Learn how to negotiate your karma.

The first step in negotiating karma is to stop performing harmful actions. We all do things knowing they are wrong. We know it is wrong to speak badly of others, to criticize, to curse. We know it is wrong to treat one another badly. Yet we do. We feel justified. We feel that it is our right. We feel that others deserve to suffer.

We get angry when we are accused. We are envious of other's looks. We are proud when we are proven right. We are afraid when we may be discovered. We are constantly, from moment to moment, in tension, because we are so under the influence of hidden motivations and impulses, and we are running from event to event, from scene to scene, always with the subtle belief that somehow we will get away with it all.

"The results are always that which speak; it serves no purpose to have good intentions if the results are disastrous." - Samael Aun Weor

Our intentions are not weighed on the scale: our actions and their results are. Therefore, we need to know how to act properly, not merely relying on our good intentions.

Do things as you would have them done to you. If you want to be treated well, then treat others well, and you create a cycle of actions and consequences. This is the fundamental way to negotiate karma: stop harmful actions, adopt beneficial ones.

If someone offends you, and does something that you consider to be really terrible, then the right action may be to forgive them and love them, and to help them without judging them or trying to tell them what you think of them.

A good example of this type of conscious action can be found in the life of Gandhi. There was a tremendous upheaval in India, and the Muslims and Hindus were killing each other. This was a very bitter and very violent civil war, and many, many people were killed and maimed. To protest this situation, Gandhi fasted, refusing to eat, because he understood that they were all unable to listen to reason, being so motivated by passionate hatred and anger.

Even though he was Hindu, he was well-loved by Muslims and Hindus alike, and so people eventually responded to his protest and stopped fighting and killing, and many, many people came to see him, lying on his bed, near dead from lack of food.

One Hindu man came to him, crying in remorse, and said he realized he had done terrible things, and he said he had killed many Muslims, and had killed even women and children. This man was deeply remorseful and asked what could he ever do to make up for it. Because he was so remorseful and recognized that he was responsible, Gandhi knew he was open to hearing. So Gandhi told the Hindu man to find a parentless Muslim child, take him as his own child, and raise him. The man eagerly agreed to this, and was very grateful. But Gandhi said, "Wait, that is not all; you must raise him as a Muslim."

Of course, this surprised the Hindu man: to raise a child of his enemy according to the ways of his enemy? This was, of course, the right thing to do.

Strong action produces strong effects. To overcome strong effects, one needs to perform even stronger actions. Remember: a superior action overcomes an inferior action.

The greatest forms of action are great acts of sacrifice, in which we sacrifice our own interests and desires in order to better serve others.

> "O My Father, if it is possible, let this cup pass from Me; nevertheless, not as I will, but as You [will]." - Jesus, Matthew 26

This is Right Action. This is conscious action. This is sacrifice, and is a beautiful example for all of us to learn from. But remember: sacrifice means we give something up. The Hindu man of our example was going to have to give up a lot: his social image, his pride, his vanity, his own religion, all for the benefit of a child, and as penance for his wrong actions...

> "Give and you shall be given. The more you give, the more you shall

be given, but whosoever gives nothing, even that which he has shall be taken away from him. - Samael Aun Weor, The Pistis Sophia Unveiled

"The sick, instead of worrying so much about themselves, should work for others, do works of charity, try to heal others, console the afflicted, take persons who cannot pay to the doctor, give away medicines, etc., and in this manner they would cancel their karma and they would be totally healed.

"Whoever suffers in their home should multiply their humility, their patience and serenity. Do not answer with insults; do not tyrannize your fellowmen, do not upset those who surround you, know how to forgive the defects of others with patience multiplied to the infinite. In this manner you would cancel your karma and would become better." - Samael Aun Weor

All of these efforts-—beginning with the moment to moment effort to observe yourself, to be conscious of everything you do and to be watching the mind very carefully—indicates to your inner Being that you are willing to change. If you demonstrate though your actions that you are willing to renounce your desires and comforts and conveniences in order to serve the greater good, then your Innermost can negotiate your karma on your behalf, thus you will receive what you need to continue in resolving your debts.

Those who are serious about activating the three factors in their moment to moment experience will gradually awaken consciousness until they are capable of another level of negotiation of karma: direct negotiation in the Temple of Karma. A student who has awakened enough consciousness can earn the right to go to the Temple of Karma in the Astral Plane, out of the physical body, and negotiate with Anubis and the Lords of Karma, to solicit credit, or ask for help.

To pay what we owe, we must perform good deeds.

We cannot perform good deeds when we are hypnotized by craving, aversion, and ignorance.

Desire causes suffering. To be free of suffering, free yourself of desire. Those beings who are free of desire become completely free from bondage, and are able to act in splendorous ways for the benefit of all beings. Yet those who are bound by desire suffer and cause others to suffer.

Karma exists to purge us of desire.

The One Law, with intense compassion for the consciousness, delivers our karma unto us as a medicine for our own good, to deliver us from our own evils. When we suffer, it is for us to learn.

The creatures who suffer in hell are there because God has compassion on them, and wants to give them another chance to reach for perfection.

The One Law punishes the formations of desire. Unfortunately, when the consciousness is trapped inside the formations of desire, the consciousness suffers when the formations of desire are punished.

The consciousness can appeal to the law for help. The consciousness can receive assistance, benefits, credits, etc from the law. However, nothing is free.

To come into harmony with the law requires that we be cleaned of all ego.

The formations of desire are opposed to the One Law. The formations of desire are the result of our past actions, and are our own karma, and bring us suffering.

To come into complete harmony with the law means to embody the law.

Karma is beyond good and evil.

Karma is the balance of action.

Within all good there is bad, and within all bad there is good.

The gods transcend good and evil. The gods embody Love, which is the law.

Karma is cognizant love in action.

> "If I speak in the tongues of men and of angels, but have not love, I am a noisy gong or a clanging cymbal. And if I have prophetic powers, and understand all mysteries and all knowledge, and if I have all faith so as to move mountains, but have not love, I am nothing. If I give my body to be burned (out of pride), but have not love, I gain nothing.

> "Love is patient and kind; love is not jealous or boastful; it is not arrogant

or rude. Love does not insist on its own way; it is not irritable or resentful; it does not rejoice at wrong, but rejoices in the right. Love bears all things, believes all things, hopes all things, endures all things.

"Love never ends; as for prophecies, they will pass away; as for tongues, they will cease; as for knowledge, it will pass away. For our knowledge is imperfect and our prophecy is imperfect; but when the perfect comes, the imperfect will pass away." - The Apostle Paul from 1 Corinthians 13:1-10

Learn to love consciously, and you will learn to live in balance with the law. Deeds, not intentions, are what count.

"For it is not the hearers of the law who are righteous before God, but the doers of the law who will be fulfilled." - The Apostle Paul from Romans 2:13

Love is the law, but conscious Love. Do what thou will, but know that thou shalt have to answer for all thy deeds.

ABOUT THE AUTHOR

Nikias Annas, whose Greek name means "victory to divine compassion," studied all major religions before discovering the Gnostic tradition of Samael Aun Weor, which radically transformed his life and gave him the keys to experiencing the reality of those religions for himself. This book is his way of showing his gratitude.

Glorian Publishing is a non-profit publisher dedicated to spreading the sacred universal doctrine to suffering humanity. All of our works are made possible by the kindness and generosity of sponsors. If you would like to make a tax-deductible donation, you may send it to the address below, or visit our website for other alternatives. If you would like to sponsor the publication of a book, please contact us at 877-726-2359 or help@gnosticteachings.org.

Glorian Publishing
PO Box 110225
Brooklyn, NY 11211 US
Phone: 877-726-2359

VISIT US ONLINE AT:

gnosticteachings.org